CREATIVE MINISTRY MOVES

by
Bishop Sir Walter Mack

Creative Ministry Moves
ISBN: 978-1-939570-70-3
E-book ISBN: 9781939570710
Copyright © 2017 by Sir Walter Mack

Published by Word and Spirit Publishing
P.O. Box 701403
Tulsa, Oklahoma 74170

Printed in the United States of America. All rights reserved under International Copyright Law. Content and/or cover may not be reproduced in whole or in part in any form without the expressed written consent of the Publisher.

TABLE OF CONTENTS

Articles and Sermons from Contributing Writers On Creativity and Ministry

Creativity In Worship
Dr. M. Keith McDaniel Sr.
Macedonia Baptist Church,
Spartanburg, South Carolina
Duke University, M.Div.
United Theological Seminary, D. Min

Creativity In Music
Pastor Kurt A. Campbell
Ignite Christian Fellowship
Creedmoor, North Carolina
Attended Shaw University,
M.Div. Candidate

The Creativity of Reaching Young Fatherless Males
Dr. John Tyus
ID Movement
Columbus, Ohio
United Theological Seminary, D. Min

Creative Youth Ministry
Dr. Kia R. Hood
Union Baptist Church, Jamestown/High Point, North Carolina
Wake Forest University, M.Div.
United Theological Seminary, D. Min

Creative Pastoral Mentoring in the Present Day Church
Pastor James H. Wilkes, Jr.
Elon Baptist Church, Elon, North Carolina
Wake Forest University- Candidate for M. Div

The Creativity of Moving From Good to Great

Pastor Kathy Dunton
St. Peters United Methodist Church
Oxford, North Carolina
Shaw University, B.A
Duke University, M.Div

The Creativity of Bible Studies

Minister Derrick Wayne Webster
Oak Ridge First Baptist Church
Oak Ridge, North Carolina
Shaw University, B.A
Masters of Divinity Candidate

The Creativity of a Christian Dance Party

Dr. Kevin D. Sturdevant
Grooms Chapel Church
Reidsville, North Carolina
Shaw University, M.Div.
United Theological Seminary, D.Min

The Politics of Jesus and Creativity

Dr. Herbert Miller
Metropolitan Tabernacle Church
Flint, Michigan
Wake Forest University, M.Div.
United Theological Seminary, D. Min

Just Program it and Watch It Go!

Reverend Latonya Oakley
Unwrapping The Gift Foundation
Oxford, North Carolina
North Carolina Central University, B.A, Masters of Psychology
Masters of Divinity Candidate

The Importance of Reaching Men in the Post Modern Era
Pastor Derrick Horton
Impact Church
Durham, North Carolina
Shaw University-B.A.,
Masters of Divinity Candidate

Creating A Plan To Move From Traditionalism To Transformation
Dr. Rodney Coleman
First Baptist Church, Chapel Hill, North Carolina
Wake Forest University, M.Div.
United Theological Seminary, D. Min

DEDICATION

I would like to dedicate this book to the best staff in the world, the Union Baptist Church Staff. The Union Baptist Church in Winston-Salem, North Carolina, would not be what it is today if it were not for you, the "Hidden Figures" in our ministry that make us all look good. Thank you for your dedication to worship, study, serve, and tolerate me! I have seen you pull off major citywide programs and events, and you did it with no complaint. You have planned prayer gatherings, conferences, social events, and the implementation of two church plants—all while still working with the demands of the people. You are amazing. The work you do from the parking lot to the pulpit is unmatched, so this book is dedicated to you, and I truly want to say, "Thank you." All of you have become my heartbeat.

I would also like to dedicate this book to the officers, leaders, volunteers, and members of Union Baptist Church. I am so thankful for your willingness to take risk and do ministry creatively. To our senior members, thank you for having a passion to stay relevant. And to our younger members, thank you for always respecting the elders. You are a church that embodies a great partnership of old and young, and let us thank God for giving us one another.

To my wife, Kim Mack, to my mother, Frances J. Mack, and to all of my family; Walteria, Clifton, Cynthia, Monica, Mark Sr., Chris, Tina, Mark, Jr., Mashad, Melia, Christina, and to my extended family in heart, thank you for inspiring creativity in me in my private time. All of you are too much fun, and I love you dearly.

THE ACKNOWLEDGMENTS

These acknowledgements are very sacred to me, because I would like to take time to recognize all of the pastors and preachers that have creatively inspired my life down through the years. To each of you God has allowed me to serve with, I want you to know that I have not forgotten all that you mean to me and how you have been a tremendous blessing to my ministry. Please take a moment and read about the moments that made me, and the many people who shaped me, to be what I am today.

* The asterisk is an indication of those who are sainted and resting with our Lord

*Dr. Sir Walter Mack, Sr.- It seems like yesterday when you left us in November of 1982. While you are resting easy with your Lord, your works here are still manifesting. Thank you for teaching me how to be a man, and I am grateful that it was under the unction of your preaching that I received Christ. It was your creative style of the sermon craft that captured me to a place of awe and moved people and preachers to often refer to you as the "silver-tongued preacher," meaning one with an extraordinary gift to preach. It was your creative approach to pastoring, loving people, and keeping the church on cutting edge that gives me inspiration to do creative ministry today. Keep on resting easy, and know that Mom, all of your children, and your grandchildren are doing quite well. **Emmanuel Baptist Church, Winston-Salem, North Carolina and the Buncombe Baptist Church, Lexington, North Carolina.**

*Dr. Benjamin Alexander Mack- I merely showed up at the Morehead Baptist Church in Durham, North Carolina, to be your youth day speaker, and it was you who put a robe on me and told me I wasn't going to speak. But I was going to *preach*. While I had not preached an initial sermon, you pushed me in the preaching waters and told me to swim. Uncle, thank you for teaching me how to creatively close a sermon and to leave people with hope and inspiration. **Morehead Baptist Church, Durham, North Carolina.**

Dr. John Mendez- Thank you for the tremendous creativity you inspired me to through social justice and preaching. Your amazing gift of speaking truth to power, and your ability to bring a text alive with relevance to biblical foundation and social analysis, has inspired me to learn more and always look for ways to do it better. **Emmanuel Baptist Church, Winston-Salem, North Carolina.**

*Reverend Julia Swindell- You served my father faithfully until his death as his Assistant Pastor, and after his demise you became the principal preacher for our congregation. And, must I add, you preached. In 1980 you took many hits because you were a female preacher, and many of the tradition didn't understand why my father would appoint you to such a position and grant you such an opportunity. But I learned from you that the preaching gift is genderless, and it is because of you I have a passion today to give women preachers a chance and open doors for them as my father did for you. Thank you for handling the craft with dignity and integrity. **Emmanuel Baptist Church, Winston-Salem, North Carolina**

*Dr. William Augustus Jones- I will never forget the day I heard you preach for the first time at Vanderbilt University. I knew after hearing you my life would never be the same. It was in that moment I was inspired to creatively tell sermon illustrations. You would share and make an attempt at creatively using words for clarity and description. Thank you for considering me to work for you at the Bethany Baptist Church in Brooklyn, New York, and mentoring me at United Theological Seminary in Dayton, Ohio. Rest in Peace - **Bethany Baptist Church, Brooklyn, New York**

*Dr. Harold Carter, Sr.- Your gift of presence in my life is immeasurable. Your passion and creativity for prayer, worship, and evangelism has become a major part of my ministry personality. As a matter of fact, our churches' declaration statement, "A Church Determined To Live For Christ," was inspired by you. Thank you also for mentoring me at United

Theological Seminary in Dayton, Ohio. **New Shiloh Baptist Church, Baltimore, Maryland**

Dr. Gardner Calvin Taylor- I called and you answered to come and be the anniversary speaker at my first church, New Hope Granville Missionary Baptist Church, Oxford, North Carolina. I will always cherish the moment we shared in the graveyard together looking for the plot of your friend Marshall Fields, who consequently was buried in that city. When we found that plot, you wept and cried. Thank you for reminding me that though the graveyard is the place that represents death, life can come out of it. This is what you creatively preached to thousands for so many years, and I am so thankful that you added life to my ministry and my life. **Convent Baptist Church, Brooklyn, New York**

Dr. C. Eric Lincoln- I met you at Duke University, and you granted me the privilege to be among ten students who would study at your feet in 1991. After your home was set on fire, a church helped you. You wanted to thank them, and you asked me to preach what you called "Help Sunday." It was the confidence you had in me that propelled me to other platforms for ministry. Thank you for letting me read the rough draft of *The Black Church and the African American Dilemma*. Today millions of people use that book for scholarship, and I still have a copy of the rough draft in my possession and will always cherish it. **Duke University, Durham, North Carolina**

Dr. Fred G. Sampson- I was merely asked by my pastor, Dr. John Mendez, to introduce you to our church for the seventy-fifth church anniversary. I was nineteen years old, and I introduced you by using an analogy from Howard Thurman, of course at the tutelage of Dr. Mendez. When I finished, you said to me, "Young man, you have a letter that you have not read yet." I considered this to be a confirmation of my prayer about ministry. Thank you for speaking into my life, and it is because of you that I quote Shakespeare, Edgar Allen Poe, Paul Lawrence Dunbar, Maya Angelou, John Oxenham, and other poets in my preaching today. Nobody could do it like you. **Tabernacle Baptist Church, Detroit, Michigan**

*Dr. Samuel Dewitt Proctor- Though my time with you was brief, it was very impactful. I was asked, as a student at Duke Divinity School, to be your host for the week. The time you rode in my vehicle, I will never forget the deliberate intent of words that you used to describe a moment. Storytelling is my take away with you, and every opportunity I get to share one in sermon compilation, I will do it. Thank you, sir. **Duke University, Durham, North Carolina.**

Dr. Charles Edward Booth- As a young seminarian I traveled two hours to hear you preach in Fayetteville, North Carolina. After that night, my preaching has never been the same. Your creativity to find nuggets in a story laced with history, information, inspiration, transparency, and passion is unmatched. You have taken the time to give criticism to my preaching, inspired me to read more, and you have even expressed some of your most sacred ministry moments with the hope I could learn from your experience. Thank you for being a big brother to me and being my revivalist for the past seventeen years at the time of this writing. God is still a healer, and that's what we claim. **Mt. Olivet Baptist Church, Columbus, Ohio**

Dr. William Watley- I simply invited you to be our lecturer at Union Baptist, not knowing that I would have very special ministry opportunities with you. William A. Curtis and I would sit at your feet once a year and listen to the words that are priceless for any practitioner of the gospel. Thank you for trusting me to teach your people and for being a mentor that I can keep it 100% percent with. Thank you for letting me reprint the chapter that I originally wrote for your book, *Doing Church*, the section titled "Church Order" in this book. **St. Phillip A.M.E. Church, Atlanta, Georgia.**

Dr. William C. Turner- My first encounter with you was at Elon College, as you were our Martin Luther King Day Speaker. At that time, I did not know that you would later become my navigator through seminary and I would become your driver to the Hampton Ministers Conference, where you were invited to be the guest lecturer. I sat on that stage with you in Ogden Hall, and I saw you creatively handle the moment. Your lecture on the "Holy Spirit" was mind blowing. Returning from Hampton, we stopped and visited another ministry icon, Dr. Miles Jones, who was working in his yard in a t-shirt. I didn't know him at that time, but after reading his writings and studying his preaching paradigm, I learned that he was a giant of the faith. I will never forget his handshake and his contribution to the kingdom. **Duke University and Mt. Level Baptist Church, Durham, North Carolina,**

Bishop Neil C. Ellis- You saw something in me that I didn't see in myself. From day one, God connected us and you spoke prophetic words in my life that are now coming to pass. Thank you for extending the Bishopric to me, for the opportunity to share with you in Global United Fellowship, and for giving me a chance to creatively share my gift globally. I am amazed at how you do it, but creating and then executing is your gift. Keep doing it; the world is waiting on it. **Mt. Tabor Baptist Church, Nassau, Bahamas, Global United Fellowship, Presiding Prelate**

Bishop J. Delano Ellis- Thank you for all of your fatherly advice during my elevation to the Bishopric. You have been a tremendous inspiration in my life, and I am eternally grateful for all you share with us.

Bishop T.D. Jakes- While we have not spent much time together, you have always made room to share you gift with my ministry. You have written an endorsement for my book, *Destined For Promotion*, you wrote a poem for my wife and I during our wedding ceremony, and you shared with our ministry during our phone-line worship at the Union Church. However, one of the greatest compliments you could have ever spoken to me is when you saw me in Phoenix, Arizona, and you shared with me that my book, *How To Make a Wrong Relationship Right*, was a great book. When you told me that you took the time to read that book, it inspired me to write more. Thank you for your creativity and innovative ways of doing ministry. We all learn from you. **Potters House, Dallas, Texas**

Bishop Noel Jones- We met during the North Carolina Consortium under the leadership of Bishop A.L. Jinwright. He connected us in ministry, as a result of that you became an intricate part of my life and ministry. Thank you for creatively teaching us how to preach. While you show a tremendous intensity at the preaching moment, you are just as intent about helping developing preachers like myself. Thank you for giving me the opportunity to share in your pulpit, and I will never forget the sacrifice you made to be a part of our wedding. **City of Refuge, Los Angeles, California**

Bishop Sylvester D. Johnson- Our families go too far back, and I shall always cherish the creativity that you had for ministry even in the '70s. You have inspired my ministry since childhood, and you were the first to refer to me as a Bishop long before it really happened. Thank you for your inspiration, and keep on creatively doing what you do. **Macedonia Worship Center, Winston-Salem, North Carolina**

Dr. Leonzo Lynch- I met you on the doorsteps of Duke University. And in a brief conversation we discovered that your father, Dr. Lorenzo Lynch, and my father had been great friends down through the years. Shortly thereafter, you invited me to preach for you, and you have been a brother to me since 1990. You then referred me to preach for many of your friends, and the doors flung open. It is through you that I have connected with so many preachers who became great friends of mine personally. Through You, I met preachers like Ricky Woods, *Bernard Morrison, *Marcus D. Ingram, *Z.D. Harris, *Ronnie Johnson, Percy Chase, James Isaac, *Terry Thomas, Charles Pettiford, Nathanial Wall, Curt Campbell, Bruce Hurst and John Wilkins, of whom Curt, Bruce, and Bishop John Wilkins have become like brothers to me. **Ebenezer Baptist Church, Charlotte, North Carolina**

Bishop James Woodson- After the death of my father, you became a beacon light for our family. You have always been an inspiration to me and to my ministry. It is from you I hear the creativity of words and the profundity of thought. Thank you for being a brother to me and introducing me to Global United Fellowship. **St. James Home of Fresh Start, Greensboro, North Carolina**

Dr. William Barber- Who would have ever thought that when I worked for you as a student intern at the North Carolina Central University Campus Ministry that you would catapult to be a prophetic voice for the world to hear at the 2016 National Democratic Convention? Your ability to share the history and historicity of race matters and political malpractice is so creatively done that it even brings your enemies to agreement. Thank you for teaching me and mentoring me to greatness. **Greenleaf Disciples of Christ, Goldsboro, North Carolina**

Bishop Walter Scott Thomas- You invited me to the think tank in Phoenix, Arizona, and my ministry and life has never been the same. It is there that you introduced me to so many different paradigms for doing ministry. While we don't talk often, you never make me feel like that's the case. Thank you for sharing your gift with the kingdom, and know that many of the creative things in our church came by way of the information you share in Phoenix. **New Psalmist Baptist Church, Baltimore, Maryland**

Dr. Richard McBride- I was a young man at Elon College when you took me in as intern. You gave me the opportunity to learn how to lead chapel and do creative programming for students. That opportunity has blessed my ministry beyond measure, and I pray that God will continue to bless you. It was because of you that I met President Jimmy Carter in Atlanta, and Georgia and Millard Fuller, the founders of Habitat For Humanity. **Elon University, Elon, North Carolina**

Dr. James Webster- I was simply standing in line at Chick-fil-A in Greensboro, North Carolina, and ironically, you heard me place my order. And while standing behind me, you heard my father's voice in my voice. When you tapped me on my shoulder, you recognized who I was. After which, you invited me to your church to preach. Since that time you have been a solid voice of wisdom in my life, not to mention that it was because of that invitation I met one of the best friends in the world, your son, Derrick Wayne Webster. He has become a brother to me, and he now travels with me doing ministry. You have creatively taught me how to use wisdom in all that I do. **First Baptist Oak Ridge, Oak Ridge, North Carolina.**

Bishop John Wilkins- Thank you for taking me in and helping to shape my ministry destiny. It was from you that I learned how to lean into the pastorate and always be optimistic about the approach. Your creativity to administrate and galvanize people is a rarity now, but you have mastered it. Thank you for sharing insight with such humor but yet with the sternness of our Lord, who is serious about the kingdom agenda. **Wake Chapel Church, Raleigh, North Carolina**

Pastor Bruce Hurst- Your dedication and mind for ministry never ceases to amaze me. You have been a true friend and brother to me, and I will always admire your creativity to master the work of rural church ministry. Nobody does it like you. Your reading repertoire is amazing, and your dedication to ministry is unmatched. I am thankful for the Sunday morning prayers that we share together. **Leach Springs Baptist Church, Raeford, North Carolina**

Dr. Robert Charles Scott- We met in the hallway of Duke University as young preachers trying to find our way, and here we are today. Thank you for being the constant friend you have been, and for speaking truth to me when required and necessary. Every David needs a Nathan. **St. Paul Baptist Church, Charlotte, North Carolina**

Pastor Kenny Moore- Your gift of preaching and survival is unmatched. Your testimony of overcoming challenges has been a beacon light for so many, and the creativity you use to convey deep thought about some of life's most complex matters is incredible. Thank you for teaching me how to be creatively transparent. **Sharon Baptist Church, Eden, North Carolina**

Minister Derrick Webster- Your exegetical interpretation and your uncanny wit makes for a tremendous blend and contribution to the kingdom of God. Your creative approach to teaching and music contribution has taught me the need for being versatile while doing ministry. Thank you for sacrificing your time to make certain that my thoughts and ideas about ministry are on target. You are a gift that the world can never place value on. We can't count that high. **Oak Ridge Baptist Church, Oak Ridge, North Carolina.**

*Ben Ruffin- Though you were not a preacher, you really were in your own right. I want to honor you and thank you for serving as a life-mentor for me in the very tender years of my life. You inspired me, encouraged me, and showed me how to approach business opportunities while placing emphasis on the power of networking. I will always cherish the day that you called me and told me to be in Raleigh, North Carolina, in shirt and neck tie, not knowing that I was about to attend a meeting with you and about fifty other people and President Bill Clinton. You kept your promise to open as many doors for me as possible, and even today, I am trying to maximize opportunities. I will always remember you, and collectively we believe you left us too soon. Rest easy.

CREATIVE SONS AND DAUGHTERS IN MINISTRY

I would like to also acknowledge the creativity of my sons and daughters in ministry, namely, Dr. Herb Miller, Dr. Keith McDaniel, Dr. Kia Hood, Dr. Edna West, Dr. Raphael Hughes, Dr. Glenda Dillard, Dr. Phylicia Piggot-Long, Dr. Stacy Kelly, Dr. Ruth Casseberry, Pastor James Wilkes, Pastors Derrick and Keisha Horton, Pastor Kurt Campbell and Gale Campbell, Pastors Robert and Melanie Hill, Reverends: Melvin Aiken, Claudette Mack, Birdie Rush, Rhon Hammond, LaKeisha Hill, Kezra Marshall, Patrick Milam, Cory Thomas, Michael Weeks, Joe Wade, DeWayne Wade, Denise Wade, Leon McCullough, Randy Brown, Stephen Stover, Tony Clark, Latonya Oakley and Andre Ruffin, David Saunders, Clarence Hairston, Jamar Gentry, *Beverly McCarthy, *Benjamin Mosely, Silas and Kaye Hart Rodney

A special recognition to two men who serve on our ministry staff; their presence in our ministry is a tremendous support to me. Thank you Dr. W.O. McCullough and Dr. Hoyt Cooper for your wisdom and guidance. Between the two of them, I am able to receive seventy years of pastoral experience and wisdom about creatively pastoring. I thank God for them both.

CREATIVE CLERGY LEADERS

There are many pastors and ministers who have given me an opportunity to serve beside them in ministry, or whom I have had a significant ministry experience with. Therefore, I would like to acknowledge them and appreciate them in this writing. Each name listed represents a personal story of my time with them, and I cherish every moment. If your name is not listed, please bring it to my attention, and I will be glad to acknowledge you in my next writing.

*A.H. McDaniel, *B.F. Daniels, *J. Ray Butler, *Isaiah Jones, *Marcus D. Ingram, Johnny Boyd, Lorenzo Lynch, Jerome Ross, John Bryant, *John Heath, George Brooks, Cardes H. Brown, J.C. Hash, Sr., *R.M. Pitts, *W.M. Adams, J.D. Ballard, *Warner C. Hay, *Warren Jake Napper, Warren Clinton Napper,*David R. Hedgley, *J. Ray Butler, *Leonard Macon, *Bracey Bonham, *Joe Nance, Robert McGowans, Carlton Eversley, Serenus Churn, James Fulwood, Konnie Robinson, *Jerry Drayton, *J.R. Samuels, *Philimon Samuels, *E.L Clark, Charles Adams, G.E. Patterson, Wyatt T. Walker, Walter Malone, Alfred Thompson, Keith Troy, *Archie Logan, *Terry Thomas, R.W. Styles, Helen Styles, Sam Cornelius, Charles Leak, *Cedric Rodney, T.R. Rice, Shirley Caesar, Al Sharpton, *J.C. Copeland, *K.O.P Goodwin, *S.E. Tyndall, *Richard Hairston, *Helen and Robert Corpening. Cynthia Hale, J. Lewis Felton, Millicent Hunter, Kent Millard, Robert Charles Scott, Bill Leonard, Barry Washington, William D. Curtis, Claybon Lee, C. Dexter Wise, John Gunns, Dennis Proctor, Chris Young, Joe Ratliff, Harold Ray, Wayne Snodgrass, Harold Carter, Jr., Carolyn Showell, Jessie Williams, Delton Ellis, Claude Alexander, Anthony Macklin, Kevin Greshen, David Evans, Lance Watson, Patricia Bailey, Brian Moore, Rudolf McKissick, Sr., Patrick Cheston, Heber Brown, Sr., Greg Moss, Jeffrey Reeves, Craig Johnson, Marvin Sapp, Leofric Thomas, Brehon Hall, A.J. Wright, Wayne Thompson, Wayne Wilson, Frank Thomas, Eric Gladney, Harold Hudson, Timothy Clark, Charles and Jennifer Maxwell, Matthew Watley, Harry White, Haywood T. Gray, Sonya Laws, Kenneth Hammonds, Sheldon McCarter, Joyce McCarter, J.C. and Lady Hash, J.C. Hash, Jr.,

Tim Forbes. Nathan Scovens, Rosa Lee Friar, Larry Covington, Yvonne Hines, Ben Hinton, Carlton Pressley, Billy Houze, Cheryl Moore, John Walker, John Parks, Dejado and Victoria Hanchell, Omar Dykes, Kendall Jones, Benjamin Mittman, Johnny Freeman, Maurice Maxwell, Lamont Williams, T.L. Carmichael, Darryl Napper, Renita Timberlake, Marvin Mitchell, Gloria Samuels, Groshun and Debra Terry Stevens, Todd Fulton, Barry Washington, Rodney Colman, Lamont Cooper, Kevin Shouse, James and Renita Linville, James Cook, Randy Cain, Joel and Valarie Bailey, Bobby Best, Greg Baker, Byron Battle, Anthony Wilson, Jerry Corpening, Ben Sutton, William Phillips, Michael Weeks, Mack McConnell, Eric Baldwin, Darryl Hairston, Lucious Dalton, Dwight Hash, Elvin Sadler, Larry Hinton, Keith Martin, William Phillips, Vashti Mckenzie, Dwight Bryant, Sam Stevenson, Pastors Robert and Mary Coleman, Pastors Richard and Helen Styles, Yvette Lovette Martin, Michael Long, Thomas Bannister, Daniel Webb, Dayhige Wright, Frank Thomas, Bryan Pierce, William Washington, Kevin Williams, Patrick Usher, Serenus Churn, Dennis Leach,*F.D. Betts, Robert Williams, Charlie Williams, Sherman Tribble, *F.D. Patterson, Ed Allen, Herbert Dickerson, Kathy Dunton, Ricky Woods, J. Vincent Terry, Harry Cohen, William Daye, Clarence Johnson, John McCullough, Norman Kerry, Paul Drummond, A.L. Jinwright, Cliff Jones, *W. T Bigelow, Timothy Lyons, Glenn Davis, Reginald Van Stevens, Victor Davis, Phillip Davis, Prince Rivers, Darryl Aaron, Larry Fitzgerald, Dianne Moffit, David Reeves, Herman Platt, Steven Williams, *Otis Lockett, Gregory Baker, *Thurman Hairston, Adrian Mouldevann, Cliff Buchram, Clarence Hairston, Matthew Johnson, Johnny Draft, *Quincy Caldwell, Derwin Montgomery, Jackie Young Moore, James Rowdy, Mattie Ingram, Toure Marshall, Freddie Marshall, Lamont Williams, Dennis Bishop, Michael Long, Joseph Parks, Wayne Wilson, James Dixon, Lawrence Cavanah, James Lewis, Lester Boyd, George Pass, Kevin Sturdevant, Marshall Walker, Dwight Steel, Reggie Sharp, E. Dewey Smith, Antionette Wright, Theodore Breeden, J.C. Harris, T.R. Rice, Carl H. Gill, Sr., Charles Gray, Barbara Petty, Donald Stowe, Maurice, Wallace, William Height, Cheryl Moore, *Jason Barr, John Jackson, William Wright,

William Epps, Buster Soaries, Randolph and Lady Bracey, Cedric Crawford, Tyrone Tyson, Kevin Gibson, Stacy Goodson, Scott Brothers and Son, Angela Harris, William Betts, Harold Trice, Ann Dalton, Reginald McCaskill, Justin Vannoy, Chris Farrabee, Claudette Mack, Steve Williams, *Earlene Parmon, Keefer Bradshaw, *A.C. Stowe, Cornelius Battle, Claude Forehand, Claude Alexander, Luther Barnes, Eddie Long, Willard Bass, Dennis George Bloomer, Johaness Christian, Eddie B. Sands, Mary and Robert Coleman, Phillip Cousins, Wesley McLaughlin, Darren Brandon, Tony Hopkins, James Smith, Gerald Moody, Derwin Montgomery, Antiwon Yowe, Derek McNair, James McKinnon, LaShonda Ely, Sylvester Patton, Selester Stuart, Albert Moses, Maurice Watson, James Graham, H. Beecher Hicks, J. Delano Ellis, Calvin Butts, James Perkins, Freddie Johnson, Lincoln Lee, Claire Phelps, Anthony Trufant, George Gibson, Liston Page, Anthony Chandler, Reggie Barnes, Evander Hughes, Kirk Whalum, Johnathan Butler, W.L. Wilson, James Clyburn, Elmer Davis, Hiawatha Hemphill, Chuck Wilson, Greg Baker, Mark Royster, Del Bronner, Ned Thorpe, Craig Ingram, Jerry Carter, Floyd Flake, Richard Lischer, James Efird, Willie Jennings, Candice Benbow, Bruce Grady, John Wilson, III, Bryant Irvin, Rebecca Carmichael, George Banks, Johnny Freeman, Reginald Barnes

While there are many more preachers that I wanted to mention who blessed me down through the years, neither time nor space would allow me that privilege. However, if you do not see your name in the list, just know that I still have not dismissed your place in my life. Bring it to my attention, and I will certainly acknowledge you in my next book.

Introduction

Creative Ministry Moves approaches the idea of mobilizing the church and church leaders to see the importance of creativity as it pertains to innovative worship, preaching, teaching, programs, evangelism, and leadership development. While this sounds very practical and simplistic in its inception, there are various and sundry factors, which must be considered in making this a reality for the church. Moving the church to innovation merits us to illuminate biblical, theological, political, social, cultural, and relational matters regarding the present day church.

The book of Acts becomes a more consistent model of establishing a focus of effective creative ministry. Whenever the apostles exercised the work of Christ, it was often done with the idea of establishing the Kingdom of God throughout a region or in a city that knew not the ways of God or the way of Christ. Therefore, the church becomes the residential force for establishing the kingdom of God, and establishing order in the government of God. Jesus places a priority on the church going outside, and bringing those outside in when he says, "Go ye therefore, and teach all nations, baptizing them in the name of the Father, Son and Holy Ghost." This ironically has become Jesus' last commandment, but it is imperative we interpret it as our first priority. Therefore, *Creative Ministry Moves* is designed to help strengthen the gates of the church, while helping the church to develop creative strategies for claiming the region in which it exist.

It was Curry Blake who once stated, "if your Gospel isn't touching others, it hasn't touched you." This idea of making the gospel real and relevant takes on various forms and functions, and this writing will introduce the power of creative programs and innovative ministry opportunities that will help churches to understand the clarion call of reaching this present-day generation. John Keith Falconer declares, "I have but one candle of life to burn, and I would rather burn it out in a land filled with darkness than in a land flooded with light."

In conclusion, it is imperative we begin to explore creative forms and practices that will give the church a new-found perspective on the power of programming ministry empowered by the preaching of the gospel, worship, and formations for winning souls to Christ.

CHAPTER 1

THE CHURCH AND CREATIVE ESTABLISHMENT

One of the realities we must recognize in the body of Christ is that God always intended for the church to be a creative force. If the church is to be the visible representation of an invisible God, then the imaginative effort of our mind about God begins with creativity. Perhaps this is why God says in the book of Genesis 1:1 "In the beginning God created the heavens and the earth." Therefore, in the beginning God created the beginning with an anticipation of the end. Because in the Old Testament, beginning (*r šît*) is often connected with the "end" (*a rît*). However, between the beginning and the end is God's sovereign work of creation, which ultimately begins with God's own creative capacity.

Creation and creativity is all in God's spoken word, and when His word is spoken it introduces new activity. Not only is there "new activity" but there is *creatio ex nihilo* ("creation out of nothing.") However, in the midst of the creation, if we are not careful we can easily get distracted and pay more attention to the creation, and negate the one and only Creator. God is the creator of the created, and it all began with creativity.

What is interesting for us to consider is that even after heaven and earth was created, earth was still unproductive and unhabituated. Which means creativity alone does not mean completion, but creativity becomes

Even though God created heaven and earth, there is still much work to be done, and much purpose to be fulfilled.

a means to get to the created. It is what the Creator uses to create.

Even though God created heaven and earth, there is still much work to be done, and much purpose to be fulfilled. This becomes the responsibility and function of the church. The role of the church has always been to image God and to be a microcosm of creation. Therefore, what we see in God, we should see in the church. What we see in the church, we see in creation. However, because God reveals Himself in creation in ways not often easily discerned, it takes creativity to see God takes nothing and creates something in the church, which is called to embody who He is. Perhaps this is what Julia Cameron tried to inspire when she said, "We ourselves are creations. We are meant to continue creativity by being creative ourselves. This is the God-force extending itself through us. Creativity is God's gift to us. Using creativity is our gift back to God." - *Heart Steps*. George Bernard Shaw said it this way, "Imagination is the beginning of creation. You imagine what you desire; you "will" what you imagine; and at last you create what you "will." (Quotable Quotes, Roy B. Zuck, p. 92, 1997, Kregal Publications, Grand Rapids, Michigan.)

Therefore, if we are going to embrace the idea of audacity and creativity, this book will consider ways to be creative in the church. If the church is to continue in the vain of God, and advance the kingdom of God with potency, relevancy, authority and boldness, the church must began to see creativity as something to embrace, and not something to be intimidated by. Creativity becomes a friend to the church, a cohort of our work, and an assistant to establishing the kingdom purpose.

There is an emerging crisis unfolding in the church today, and the crisis is that many churches have long forgotten God at the core is a creative power, a creative being who draws His strength from creativity. This is what is so needed today in the church, the ecclesia, the body of Christ. Because it seems in many ways, the omnipotence of God, and all that God has the potential to be for many, has been diminished by our lack of exploration and openness to creativity.

All research data, and the diminishing numbers we see as pastors and church leaders will clearly reflect there is something going on today, when the church is now leaving the church. I'm not speaking of leaving in regards to evangelism, or church leaving the church to witness, but it is becoming more apparent in many ways the church is not even going to church. There are many churches doing quite well with attendance, and may not have a problem with the "empty pew" Sunday. It is important before you celebrate, you remember your church is not "the Church," you are a branch on the tree. But if we were to do an examination of the tree at its root, honesty would have us to confess the bark is falling off of the tree, and decay has set in, and it just looks like the tree is dying. The church is leaving the church. This is a concern that is spreading throughout the nation that has many pastors and church leaders raising questions and asking, "Where are the church members this Sunday morning?"

The best way I can describe this experience is one Sunday while driving to the church along my regular route, I saw cars taking an alternate route. I wasn't quite sure what was taking place ahead of me, but when I approached closer, I discovered there was a detour sign directing us another way. When I followed the detour sign, shortly thereafter, I noticed the detour sign was there because there was a marathon race taking place on Sunday morning. There were hundreds of people in the race on Sunday morning at a time when traditionally people would be in church. It occurred to me, there is a detour sign set up directing people from the church today, and while the marathon was running a race, there are many people today who are literally running from the church. Regardless of

There is a crisis taking place today in the church, and it appears as if the church is leaving the church.

what city you live in, just leave the church one Sunday morning at the time of worship and drive past the nearest Wal-Mart, Home Depot, Lowes, Starbucks, AAU Basketball Court, or youth dance club auditorium and don't be surprise if you find people who were once in church now replacing church with activity that has nothing to do with God.

There is a crisis taking place today in the church, and it appears as if the church is leaving the church. What is happening today that people don't value church, feel as if they don't need the church, and in some way, haven't even thought about the church? Consider these striking statistics as we prepare to engage the idea of creative evangelism.

- 83% of Americans are not attending a conventional church on the weekend.
- 80% of all churches in North America have reached a plateau where no growth is happening, and the growth that is happening is coming from what they know as switchers. "Switchers" are people who leave one church and simply join another church. This does not dictate Christian growth, as much as it does individual church growth.
- Every year, approximately 4000 new churches open their doors. Every year approximately 7000 churches close their doors for the last time.[10]

One particular denomination did a survey on its leadership ministries. The results are as follows:

- 63% of the leadership in this denomination, including deacons and elders, have not led one stranger to Jesus in the last two years through the method of "Go Ye" evangelism.

- 49% of the leadership ministries spend zero time in an average week ministering outside of the church.

- 89% of the leadership ministries have zero time reserved on their list of weekly priorities for going out to evangelize.

- 99% of the leadership ministries believe every Christian, including leadership, has been commanded to preach the gospel to a lost world.

- 97% believe if the leadership had a greater conviction and involvement in evangelism, it would be an example for the church to follow.

- 96% of the leadership believe their churches would have grown faster if they would have been more involved in evangelism. Because of this, our results in evangelism have been mediocre, at best. "Street Level Evangelism by Michael Parrott, *Acts Evangelism*, Spokane, WA, 1993, pp. 9-11.

This is the reality we are facing today, and if there is anytime the church must seriously contemplate and engage critical thought and analysis about the direction of the Christian church, and even the future existence of the Christian faith, we must be willing to engage in what Cornell West calls a "Socratic Thought Process," whereby we raise questions while being vulnerable enough to realize there may not be easy answers. However difficult it may be to arrive at answers about the falling away from church, Dr. King said it best when he stated, "Rarely do we find men and women who are willing to engage in hard solid thinking. There is almost a universal quest for easy answers and half backed solutions, nothing pains some people more than having to think." If we can't solve it, at least let's begin to think about new and fresh approaches we can take to ministry, which will at least serve as a testimony that the church tried to do something. Therefore, to begin our journey it is critical the church begin looking at the necessity of creativity, and a formation for making a connection between creativity and evangelism.

CHAPTER 2

THE RELEVANT CALL FOR THE CHURCH: ITS PRESENT TEMPTATION

It is in the book of Acts, God creatively establishes what we know as the church. While it is in Acts we actually find the formation of the Church, the historical connectivity of the church actually happens when Jesus speaks the purpose of the church in the life of its disciple Peter.

Peter has already proven himself as a fisherman, but Christ charges him to fulfill the mission of fishing, not just for fish, but fishing for souls. It was Peter who was recognized by Jesus because of his revelation knowledge about who Christ was. There was a time when Jesus raised a question before his disciples in what I perceive to be a classroom setting when he asked the question, "Who do men say that I am?" While the other disciples could not answer this questioning correctly, it was Peter who got revelation and said "Thou art the Christ." It was predicated upon this revelation Jesus then says, "Peter, upon this rock, I will build my church, and the gates of hell shall not prevail." Now when Jesus speaks of the church being built upon Peter, He is not speaking about a physical church, but he is referring to the principles of holiness, miracles, revelation, power, and faith that shall come by way of the leadership and the integrity of Peter.

However, Peter is not going to be able to carry such a responsibility without experiencing temptation by the tempter, who exists to steal, kill, and destroy. Consider what Jesus says to Peter as he is facing a great temptation by the hand of Satan. In Luke 22:31, Jesus says to Peter, "Simon, Simon, Satan has desired to sift you as wheat, but I have prayed for you, for your faith not to fail."

What is the theological/spiritual implication made here? Well it could indicate that Satan understood the capacity Peter was called to. Never forget Satan is a "to and from" creature, who is everywhere in general, and nowhere in particular. Satan had enough insight to realize that his worst nightmare was wrapped up inside Peter, and to prevent having to deal with the power force of the church later, Satan understood he would need to sift Peter as wheat now. The sifting of wheat was often a process which would involve wheat being placed upon a grate with all the dirt and grime from the field on the same grate. In order to sift the wheat, the farmer would often shake the grate until the dirt and the grime falls through the screen leaving nothing but the wheat on top. It seems today Satan is sifting the church. What is happening when more pastors are being murdered in their churches today than we can ever remember hearing of in recent times? What is happening when a gunman can walk into a Bible study and murder nine Christians in the name of racism? It seems the church is going through a sifting when YouTube, social media blogs, twitter and Instagram are full of insults and attacks against the body of Christ. Sifting is all too popular today, when the church has to preach doctrine foreign to the Christian narrative or you will be labeled with preaching hate, and could possibly lose a tax-exempt status. The church is going through a sifting. The members are being sifted. Depression is all to high in the church, divorce is running rampant, and drugs are destroying young deacons before they even have a chance to finish high school. Satan desires to sift us, but Jesus said, "Peter, it won't work because I have prayed for you."

Here is the Halleluiah, Jesus prayed for Peter and somebody is praying for us.

When Jesus pronounced the church would be built upon Peter, this was the first time in history the church was contingent on one person outside of Christ. Peter had the arduous task of representing the church, and all that we are, the principles of salvation, holiness, miracles, revelation, power, and faith. The reason this was the only time in history when the church was contingent upon one person is because what happened at Pentecost made it impossible for the church to be contingent upon one individual. Pentecost eradicated individualism; as a matter of fact, the power of God was so present at Pentecost, when Peter preached 3,000 souls got saved in one day. It always amazes me there are those who would think they are the only ones God can use to do something in the church. The work is too great for you to have a "Peter Complex" where you believe the church is just contingent on you. The Holy Spirit diversifies the power, it makes the church a shared responsibility with shared ability. This is why it is going to take "the church," the entire body of Christ to tackle the challenge the church is facing. It is going to take every denomination, every region, every city where churches are comprised to address this issue of the church falling away from the church. Collectively this must happen for the preservation of the faith, considering that when the church is under attack, the faith is under attack. When one church is wounded, we all are wounded. When one church is exposed, we all are exposed. It is the Holy Spirit who unifies us, and gives us the authority to be victorious in all we seek to accomplish.

The Holy Spirit diversifies the power, it makes the church a shared responsibility with shared ability.

God has established the church through Peter, but the establishment was for the world. This same church exists today, though there are many factions of the church, we all exist bearing God's purpose and demonstrating God's power. However, creativity comes into play, when we understand we have charge to make God become alive in the lives of people. Could it be there is a falling away from the church because we lack creativity, creativity to vision, explore, analyze, connect, establish, build, and preserve? Essentially at the end of the day, we can't blame the world from falling away from the church; we must begin to self-examine, and find our area of weakness and begin there in addressing this present problem of church flight.

The Need For A Creative Church

One of the most fascinating minds that explored the sociology of religion and the practice of the African American church was the most notable C. Eric Lincoln. Dr. Lincoln in a lecture at Duke University, presented an introspective look at the creative genius of the "Invisible Institution." The "Invisible Institution" was a way of depicting black religion under a system of slavery and oppression. In this most memorable lecture, Dr. Lincoln took time to give a descriptive look at the creative efforts the slaves took to enter into worship as a protest against the system of oppression. Lincoln talked emphatically about how the slaves would wait until midnight, then sneak away from the big house and go down by the river. When they would go down by the river, they would often take blankets with them they would dip in the river water. After dipping these blankets in the river, they would then hang the blankets on the trees in a circle formation to create somewhat of a makeshift sanctuary down by the river. The reason and the purpose for the blankets on the trees is serve as a sound buffer during the moment of worship. What the slave worshipper knew is that when what E. Franklin Frazier calls the "frenzy" or the "shout" would break out, the blankets would trap the sound, so their hollers and screams could not reach "masters house" from the "river side." John Watson in his writing *Methodist Error or Friendly Advice to Those Methodist Who Indulge in Extravagant Religious Emotions and Bodily Exercises* (1819) describes the creativity even in their singing when he says, "With every word sung, they have a sinking of one or other leg of the body alternately; producing an audible sound of the feet at every step, and as manifest as the steps of actual negro dancing...If some in the meantime sit, they strike the sounds alternately on each thigh...(Slave Religion, Raboteau, p. 67,).

This kind of creativity was exemplified through their songs and even in their preaching. The slave preacher often times did not have the privilege of reading, so the oppression of the system would extend to the oppressed even reading the Bible to the oppressed. So the preacher had to be creative enough to hear the biblical story, and then act out the story in a way the congregation would get the story and understand. So if the preacher were preaching Jonah in the belly of the whale, he would literally bend over and act is if were in the belly, and then jump out as if he were being spat of the mouth of the whale. If the congregation understood the story, there was a response. The preacher would preach - that was the call, and the congregation would respond - that was the response. Hence, in the African American church there is what is called the creative participation of call and response. Translated today as, "let the church say amen," "preach preacher," "touch your neighbor" or "do I have a witness?"

This kind of creative motif in preaching, gave way to the churches having creative worship and fellowship moments like Easter sunrise services in cemeteries, all night prayer lock-ins, homecoming celebrations, revivals, men and women conferences,

> *The church must be careful in our quest to relevant and real and that we do not replace worship with evangelistic entertainment.*

healing services, and cake bakes, just to name a few of the ways the old church sought to be creative. Today, these forms of worship and fellowship are most common, and now the church is forced to think of new and innovative ways to make church practical, relevant, and meaningful. Marva Dawn in her book, *Royal Waste of Time*, says the church must be careful in our quest to relevant and real and that we do not replace worship with evangelistic entertainment. She stated, "I am convinced that we should be using new music and new worship forms; however, we use them not to attract people, but because they are faithful in praising God and forming us to be His people." (Royal Waste of Time, Marva Dawn, P.123) She goes on in this survey and makes a striking distinction between evangelism and worship. I applied what she offered this way. When I introduce my wife to the world, I will tell the world she is beautiful, wonderful, responsible, caring, and nurturing. But when she comes home from work, I don't speak to her in those terms. I want to know what her day was like, who hurt her feelings, what things happened that day that mattered and what didn't happen. In other words, when she comes home, I intimately enter into her world without interruption. Hence, Evangelism is presenting God to the world, like He is beautiful, wonderful, caring, and nurturing, but worship is to intimately engaging God as I engage my wife, with conversation and presence without interruption. "Worship is the language of love and growth between believers, and evangelism is the language of introduction between those who believe and those who don't. This understanding and distinction of worship and evangelism is revolutionary for me as it pertains to our purpose for creative ministry in the first place. It should be our goal and purpose to move people from past passivity to an active relationship with God, and worship becomes the central conduit in which that happens. Therefore, all other creative programs and various ministries are merely the arms that support the weight of worship.

CHAPTER 3

THE CULTURAL DEMAND FOR CREATIVITY: POST MODERNISM AND THE NEED FOR A CREATIVE CHURCH

Postmodernism is not easily defined because of the areas and various disciplines it embraces. Post-modernism shapes how we understand and interpret religion, literature, art, film, politics, marketing, and branding. Post Modernism is not a new phenomenon, but it merges out of modernism. However, to better understand modernism and post-modernism, it is important for us to explore pre-modernism. Premodernism preceded modernism, and it was during an era when every one believed in a diety, a god or gods. What made this era of pre-modernism so significant it is because there was uncompromising loyalty to one's god or gods. The realtionship of these gods or god was clearly defined with expectation and results. What made premodernity so significant in terms of their belief in the supernatural, is pre-modernity relied on their teachers to teach them the way. Consequently, they began to see their gods or god as their mentors and teachers saw God. In fact, the teachers became the truth, and they were absolute in their posture. This is pre-modernity. (Royal Waste of Time, Marva Dawn, p.41)

Modernism, which came out of the 1800's of Western Europe with the central focus promoting a progressive and prosperous society, elevated human reason, human progress, and human authority. "Modernism is often pictured as pursuing truth, absolutism, linear thinking, rationalism, certainty, the cerebral as opposed to the effective, the natural as opposed to the supernatural—which in turn breeds arrogance, and inflexibility, the lust to be right, the desire to control. The "enlightenment movement" and the "science movement" are actually synonymous. Science began to give humans the possiblity of controling their futures and shaping their own destiny. " Consequetly, a 'tower of Babel' was built on the ground floor of science, with technology and economics comprising the next two floors." Science began to find ways to combat ignorance, superstitions and poverty in a never-ceasing spiral of progress. (Dawn, p.42.)

As Modernism would grow as an empire, and people were being convinced we had the authority and power to reason our way to progress, and make things better. Post-moderns emerge with a new challenge and a new assignment to deconstruct what moderns built. "The modern fantasy was built on shaky foundations, without adequate checks on who controlled power. The euphoria of the myth of progress began to give way to despair….the twentieth century unfolded into major world wars, severe economic depressions, the callous violence of Hitler, the world changing terror of Hiroshima, the assassinations of leaders and the massive betrayal of government in the United States." (Dawn, p. 42). When the modern fantasy land came to a halt, the post-modern comes along and says, we must try things another way. However the first assignement for the post modern was to established there is no absolute truth, and we must know truth for ourselves. The deconstruction of the pre-modern understanding of the supernatural, and the warped system of progress by the modern must go. Phillip Sampson in his book, "The rise of post-modernity" says post-modernism is much like channel surfing. "Channel surfing with the remote control illustrates the postmodern condition: from distance the viewer experiences no plot, but merely disconncected images and shattering of feelings." (Dawn, p. 43). Louis A. Sass, in his book *Madness and Modernism: Insanity in the light of Modern Art, Literature, and Thought,* says post modernism has moved people from alienation of the 1960's to schizophernia or multiphrenia "Where by there are (a legion of selves with no constant core of character...)." In other words, there is no home in a sense, no narrative, no story that will clearly define who the post-modern is. Hence, for the post-modern there is always this search for identity and constant shifts with fads and fashions. Because there is no identity, there is also now the deconstruction of commitment and relationships. My wife who works in Human Resources gave me insight on the new employee, who really desires to work for as long as the work is working for them. The commitment level is different than the pre-moderns and moderns, the understanding of authority is different, in the basic understanding of what it means to be on time for work is different for the modern and the post-modern. Their interaction in relationships is much like "channel surfing," my stability and my commitment to this channel is as long as the effectiveness of its entertainment. "Keep entertaining me so that I don't have to deal with me, face my complexities, my conditions, or my own true reality". "Thus the post modern condition has moved people from both the premodern confidence in authorities and the modern confidence in self (autonomy) to the decentering of both self and society in a contemporary culture" (Dawn, p.44)

"Postmodernism, by contrast, recognizes how much of what we 'know' is shaped by the culture in which we live, is controlled by emotions and aesthetics and heritage, and in fact can only be intelligently held as part of a common tradition, without overbearing claims to be true or right."[1] Postmodernism, then, is not contrary to modernism, but it is a movement that comes "after" it. Modernism is defined by the Bible as being the authority of truth, God through Jesus Christ is the way. Science, knowledge and reason are the path to enlightenment. Policies and procedures are the way we

Because Postmodernism is merging realty, and those generations that are steeped in the modern tradition are quickly fading away, it is apparent the church must recognize the need for more creativity in the church.

understand protocol and systems. Postmodernism, on the other hand, is defined by values based on what feels right. Truth is relative to the individual, and what makes sense, may not have been understood historically, but it is what feels good for the "now." While moderns approach situations with answers, post moderns are not afraid to approach life with questions

Because Postmodernism is a merging realty, and those generations that are steeped in the modern tradition are quickly fading away, it is apparent the church must recognize the need for more creativity in the church. Creative churches are emerging everywhere, and they are being examples through innovative worship settings, use of paintings, drawings, YouTube video clips, game show themes, dance ministry and even exercise health efforts. These new and creative forms do not mean to excuse or dismiss the more traditional forms of doing church, but creativity should add to the more traditional values, the storytelling of the church, the preaching and teaching, and the historical refrences to homecoming and church anniversaries. Post-modernism is about being relevant, and if the church is going to be effective today and reach a generation that is ever moving and changing, then it behooves the church to be open and embrace post-modernism and creativity.

An example of creativity gripped me when I recently watched on television a story about a mother who was frantic about the possibility of losing her twin children. This mother who lives in Massachusetts accidently left her vehicle running while making a quick check back into her home. When she looked around her car was rolling down the hill with her two girls still in the car. This mother was so frantic she started running towards the car before the car rolled off a cliff. However creatively, the mother decided to first out run the car, and then get in front of the car, as if to say, if my two children are going to die, it will be over my dead body. But then instantaneously this mother uses her creative genius and decides to get down in front of the car, and become a speed bump for the car. The car rolls over her, while she served as a speed bump. As the car bumps over her, the bump is just enough to not only slow down the car, but completely stop the car; needless to say her children are alive today.

This speaks to the post modern church because many would consider this millennial/hip hop generation is in a runaway car, and the direction of the fate is total lost. If this is the opinion of many in the church today, then what creative methods can the church construct that will serve as a speed bump for the runaway generation. How does the church combat a postmodern ethos that says, "We can love Jesus and hate the church." "Who needs God when we have Google?" "Can I just have God alone and not deal with people?" The speed bump that is needed demands careful scrutiny and understanding of the present day culture. It cannot be an easy answer and a half baked solution, but must be watched, studied, prayed over, discussed, and met on with the people in whom we are trying to creatively meet. The end result for anyone who is serious about doing creative ministry should be that a car rolling uncontrollably with our future generation in it is stopped, and those who are in the uncontrolled direction are ultimately saved.

1. Carson, D. A., *Becoming Conversant with the Emerging Church*, Grand Rapids: Zondervan, 2005, p. 27.

2. Gibbs, Eddie and Ryan K. Bolger, *Emerging Churches*, Grand Rapids: Baker Academic, 2005, p. 230.

3. McLaren, Brian, *A Generous Orthodoxy*, Grand Rapids: Zondervan, 2004, p. 230.

4. http://www.christianpost.com/article/20071204/30332_2007_ Trends_Analysis:_Americans _Reformulating_Christianity.htm.

5. Gibbs and Bolger, p. 73-74.

10 Principles For Understanding the Post-Modern

Material Interpreted from "Preaching to a Post-Modern World,"
by Graham Johnston

1. Post-Modernism has at its root desirability. Truth is relative to how one sees the world, and matters connected to the heart. Post-Modernism can be inter-generational. It is a mindset in some instances that adapts one to a life style.

2. Post-Modernism brings a sense of cosmic connectedness to life and the universe. Nature and what is natural to others should not be scrutinized, but should be embraced because it is their truth. People must learn to coexist.

3. Post-Moderns live on the lighter side, and for them simple are more preferred. "Complexity is out, and simple is in." Southwest Airlines has no assigned seats, just groups. No hubs, and the planes fly the shortest distance between two points. Simplicity saves the passenger time, and the company money. (Simple Church, Rainer and Geiger, p.11).

4. Post-Moderns thrive on being individual and community simultaneously. They desire for the world to appreciate their individuality, but simply being together, and talking about life helps them to know they are not alone.

5. Post-Moderns are convinced the government, the institutional church, education, and other forums have failed them. Thus, they are forced to figure things out on their own, and sometimes it comes by way of having technology always somewhere close by to help them.

6. Post-Moderns view time as commodity. They have little time to waste in long worship services, with no takeaways. This is the gen-

eration that created the Apple watch to replace even the Rolex. Time is commodity.

7. Post-Moderns embrace a sense of transparency. While one must be mindful of what William Smith calls "ecclesiastical nudity," where transparency is given without what is tasteful, transparency helps the Post-modern to connect to another identity that becomes real for them.

8. "Post-Modernity struggle with justice. Without a wholly other God, all that is left is a world of imperfection and compromise." (Preaching to the Post-Modern World, Graham Johnston, 115.) They desire to find ways to make things right.

9. Post-Moderns embrace multi-sensory preaching. Because it appeals to the five senses; ear, eye, touch, smell, and taste. Creative methods must be explored to apply this concept to preaching.

10. Dr. Will McRaney reveals some interesting facts about Post Moderns and their faith journey: Reaching People Under 40, While Keeping People Over 60, Hammet and Peirce, P. 128)

   - Membership is meaningless and denominationalism is not very important
   - They like multiple encounters rather than single ones
   - Listener centered rather than witnessed centered
   - Dialogical rather than monological
   - Gospel story rather than presentation of gospel principles
   - Stories are more effective than propositions
   - Community integration rather than isolation
   - Consideration rather than argumentation
   - More supernatural than natural
   - More time spent planting seeds than reaping the harvest

CHAPTER 4

CREATIVE MINISTRY AND CHURCH LEADERSHIP

I first published this material in the book,
"Doing Church" by Dr. William Watley.
I am thankful for his support of this book and his permission to use in the writing.

One of the elements of ministry that is a necessity for "Creative Church" in the twenty-first century is to give honor and reverence to the place of "order" in the church. It is important order is put in proper context because in many churches either order is lifted up over any other function of ministry, or order is treated as something optional, obsolete, and not necessary for "Creative Church."

Order is derived from the Latin word *ordo-inis*, which means methodical in its structure, or in its verb form it means "to arrange" which is derived from the word *ordinare*. Theologically, God has a methodical arrangement for the church, and the effectiveness of the church is often measured by how the church extends, exercises, and interprets the order God established for the church in its inception. Alexander Pope once declared "order is heaven's first law." If this perception holds any merit of truth, then it becomes obvious order should be one of the primary laws, if not the very foundation for any ministry serious about "Creative Church."

While I believe having order in the church is vital for the function of ministry, my opinion about this matter derives from a very personal experience during my tenure of ministry. Upon graduating from the Duke Divinity School at the age of 26, I was called to pastor a rural church in North Carolina. Although this church had experienced progressive ministry in its 106-year history, upon my immediate arrival I detected a church that was severely out of order. The lack of order in this church manifested itself during my first church meeting when contention and conflict erupted to the point reprehensible anger and clear profane language were expressed, even during the benedictory prayer of that meeting. The divergence centered around a deacon who had tremendous influence in the church. Not only did he have influence, this deacon also had an indeterminate amount of responsibilities; he served as trustee, treasurer, Sunday school superintendent, and not to mention he was a relative to many of the members in the church. As a result, this deacon would often defy order by implementing his plan for the church, instead of acknowledging the church's plan. Consequently, confusion and strife manifested among many of the members, and indeed, much of it deviated from his ability to control ministry direction. His interpretation of order was "whoever has the money, determines the order." This self-determinate factor alone gave him precedence when it came to order because he was the overseer of all the church funds.

Over a period of time this kind of operation became arduous for me as the pastor, and also unbearable for many of the other officers and members of the church. In fact, this predicament only worsened as there was sure evidence of integrity violation with misappropriate handling of money, an abuse of authority and position, and even more, a shameless display of stubbornness marked with an intentionally disrespectful spirit and attitude. Soon after, this "church leader" was confronted by myself, officers, and the congregation about truth and transparency of his actions.

His ambivalent conduct became hostile and elevated. This belligerent display of defamed behavior produced an intense level of negative emotions throughout the ministry.

Irrefutably, this one member convinced five others into driving a wedge between the membership. This out-of-order group was cause for premature dismissal of meetings due to unruly conduct, interruption of church worship services because of ungodly behavior, and finally a resorted movement to have under-cover sheriff deputies in attendance at Sunday morning services because of the possible threat of gun violence. These insidious and begrudging acts not only affected the body of Christ, but in fact caused bifurcation and division between family members and life-long friends. The church was despairingly out of order. To add impact to injury, the church ended up in court with a judge making a recommendation to this group of six if they did not want to abide by the desires of the majority, they needed to consider leaving, and they did. When this splintered group left the church, the church began to blossom and grow exponentially. The spirit of the church shifted from a feeling of malignancy to a feeling of ministry. Worship services were filled with power, evangelism took a new thrust. The finances went into overflow because trust and accountability was in place, not to mention the unsaved desired to be saved.

When the church began to operate in the realm of walking in order, they witnessed a new way of "doing church" that truly gave God honor and glory.

When order was taught, explained and demonstrated, the church was able to witness God bring light out of darkness, clarity out of confusion, peace out of perplexity, and provide order out of chaos. This accomplishment did not happen by osmosis, but there were many intentional actions that took place so "order" could prevail. Through preaching and teaching about "order," the church began to look at matters differently, and understood much of what manifested upon my arrival was a direct result of things that were out of order *prior* to my arrival. As a new pastor, I perceived it to be monumental if we were going to "do church" we were going to "do church" with order. Therefore, in the transition from "disorder" to "order" emphasis had to be placed on the church understanding divine laws and principles that collaborate with being a church that possessed order. When the church began to operate in the realm of walking in order, they witnessed a new way of "doing church" that truly gave God honor and glory for the things God had done. All because they understood a new revelation about order and the proven benefits that followed.

Therefore, this chapter will focus on how we "do church" and how we do it with order. What is the intent of order? What causes the lack of order? Who does failure of order affect? What are the benefits of order? How do we establish order, and what are some of the practical ways to implement order in the church?

A Place of Violation and Establishment of Order

[1] And the entire congregation lifted up their voice, and cried; and the people wept that night. [2] And all the children of Israel murmured against Moses and against Aaron: and the whole congregation said unto them, Would God that we had died in the land of Egypt! Or would God we had died in this wilderness! [3] And wherefore hath the LORD brought us unto this land, to fall by the sword, that our wives and our children should be a prey? Was it not better for us to return into Egypt? [4] And they said one to another, Let us make a captain, and let us return into Egypt.

[5] Then Moses and Aaron fell on their faces before all the assembly of the congregation of the children of Israel. [6] And Joshua the son of Nun,

and Caleb the son of Jephunneh, *which were* of them that searched the land, rent their clothes: [7] And they spake unto all the company of the children of Israel, saying, The land, which we passed through to search it, *is* an exceeding good land. [8] If the LORD delight in us, then he will bring us into this land, and give it us; a land which floweth with milk and honey. [9] Only rebel not ye against the LORD, neither fear ye the people of the land; for they *are* bread for us: their defense[a] is departed from them, and the LORD *is* with us: fear them not. [10] But all the congregation bade stone them with stones. And the glory of the LORD appeared in the tabernacle of the congregation before all the children of Israel.

[11] And the LORD said unto Moses, how long will this people provoke me? And how long will it be ere they believe me, for all the signs which I have shewed among them? [12] I will smite them with the pestilence, and disinherit them, and will make of thee a greater nation and mightier than they.

If there is any passage of Scripture that exemplifies the establishment of order and the violation of order all in the same moment is the experience that is written in Numbers 14:1-13. In this passage Moses has already received the report from Joshua and Caleb about the land that was flowing with milk and honey, a place called Canaan. Israel had everything they needed to possess the land, with the exception of confidence to do it. Their confidence was diluted by what they saw, not what they knew. What they knew is in Numbers 13:2, God releases Moses to obtain the land, to take it and possess it. Moses follows the plan by sending one leader from each tribe on this mission see the future possession and return with a report. Among the spies were two men by the name of Joshua who represented the tribe of Ephraim and Caleb, who was a descendent from the tribe of Judah. The assignment was to investigate the land to find out the defensive ability of the Canaanites, while also

---

[a] defence: Heb. shadow

finding a place for agricultural advancement. When the Israelites arrived at the land, they indeed saw land flowing with milk and honey, cities that were large and fortified, and inhabitants who appeared as giants. After forty days, the spies went back to Moses carrying with them grapes from the Valley of Eschol. These grapes served as a symbol the land had great harvest and prosperity. This was their land to possess; however, it was with what they saw that took them off of their destined course of possessing what God had already promised. They saw the occupants of the land, the descendants of Anak as giants, and themselves as grasshoppers, (Numbers 13:30-33), and therefore rejected the opinion of Joshua and Caleb to overtake the land, but rather retreated in their desire to go back to Egypt and insulate themselves in slavery.

This reality surfaces in Numbers 14, where we find the Israelites organizing a hostile church conference with the top agenda item of the day is to do nothing but reject the plan Moses, Aaron, Joshua and Caleb are suggesting. This rejection is apparent because verse 1-3 declares... *And all the congregation lifted up their voice, and cried; and the people wept that night.* *2 And all the children of Israel murmured against Moses and against Aaron: and the whole congregation said unto them, Would God that we had died in the land of Egypt! Or would God we had died in this wilderness!* *3 And wherefore hath the LORD brought us unto this land, to fall by the sword, that our wives and our children should be a prey? Was it not better for us to return into Egypt?* It was the congregations' desire to go back to captivity rather than follow the vision, follow the plan God had given them, and possess the land God had promised. William Faulkner declared, "The past is dead and buried. In fact, it isn't even the past." (Walter Earl Fluker, *Ethical Leadership-The Quest for Character, Civility, and Community*, Fortress Press, Minneapolis, p. 61). They chose to defy the order, and "do church" the way they wanted to "do church" - they wanted to stay in the past. Defying order is not the same as confronting an issue. Confronting an issue may be done to get clarity, to be more informed about details, to make certain the task is in our ability, and can be done with a very cooperative spirit. One should never diminish healthy confrontation. As a matter of fact, invite it sometimes. However, healthy confrontation is not the same as a defiance of order. Let us consider a few elements that led to this obvious revolt and abandonment of God's order to possess what was theirs to have.

The Violation of Order Always Begins With A Murmur

This moment of the congregation "murmuring" against the direction that Moses was taking is very real and operative in ministries today. The murmuring Israel offered up was synonymous to a lament, and it stemmed not only from the fear of facing the giants in Canaan, but it seems to be more that Israel is murmuring because while they have come out of Egypt, it is apparent Egypt has not come out of them. In other words, they had on band aids from Egypt, but the wounds never healed. There is a popular thought in identity dialogue that declares, "Hurting people, often hurt people." Israel was hurting because their options were limited, they felt their snatching and quick deliverance out of Egypt was not rewarded by a place where they had to labor to obtain. In other words, if we are going to have to fight giants, we may as well labor like slaves in Egypt.

Egypt a place of stripping identity, is now their desired place for identity. They now desire to become what they once despised. To add impact to injury, the only vision they had of themselves was to see themselves dead. *Would God that we had died in the land of Egypt! Or would God we had died in this wilderness!* How could they see a way to possess a land that was flowing with milk and honey, when they only view they had of themselves were their bodies in caskets? Erich Fromm calls this necrophilia, or lovers of death. According to Fromm, "necrophiles are fascinated with all that is not alive, all that is dead; corpses, decay, feces, dirt...and they come to life primarily when they can talk about death. They tend to dwell in the past, not in the future, and are enamored by force and violence, which supplants sexuality and spiritual relations with visions of power and conquest" ((Walter Earl Fluker, *Ethical Leadership-The Quest for Character, Civility, and Community*, Fortress Press, Minneapolis, p. 74,).

Israel was not just depressed, but they were tomb-stone depressed, and now their depression is surfacing through their murmuring.

This action is most likely to happen in churches especially when there are members who practice what psychologists call "displaced emotions," where someone's experiential hurt and pain is transferred on to someone else. The resurfacing of an emotional injury often provokes this action. In other words, the low self image and the institutionalized oppression that had been an intricate part of Israel's enslavement in Egypt, all of that anger is now being transferred on to Moses, Aaron, Joshua and Caleb because they all saw life, but Israel was in love with death. Recently, I had to pray for a friend of mine because she had a rare attack on her body where suddenly she became deathly ill, and for days lived life from a life support machine. She had an acute rare illness that caused an auto immune response to her body system where the body began eating up the body. Cells began to kill off other cells, and organs began to fight against one another. Here in this instance, Israel has spiritual illness where they are fighting against themselves, working against themselves and it all surfaced through them lifting their voices in a murmur.

> *"Antagonists are individuals who, on the basis of no substantive evidence, go out of their way to make insatiable demands.*

Kenneth C. Haugk in his book, "Antagonist in the Church," refers to people who murmur as antagonist. "Antagonists are individuals who, on the basis of no substantive evidence, go out of their way to make insatiable demands, usually attacking the person or performance of others. These attacks are selfish in nature, tearing down rather than building up, and are frequently directed against those in leadership capacity." (Kenneth C. Haugk, Antagonist in The Church: How To Identify and Deal With Destructive Conflict, Augsburg Press., Minneapolis, p.21-22)

Consider some of the traits of antagonist/murmurs in the church:

- Antagonist will often demonstrate a change in how they interact with you when they don't agree with you.
- Antagonist often come with general concerns of others, which at times may be interpreted as their own anger.
- Antagonist will often ask questions about detail, want to know about financial matters to the penny, and about details as it pertains to the next move of the ministry.
- Antagonist often very manipulative in harnessing support around their issue. They are often charismatic, and have a way of attracting people who feel as they feel.
- Antagonist will often gather secret meetings, spread rumors, and attack vision without having factual or exhaustive information about what they are meeting on.
- Antagonist will often criticize leadership and the direction of the ministry openly, and will protest quietly but loudly with their withdrawal from activities and other important moments in the ministry. (Haugk, p. 81-82).

The sole intent of the "antagonist or murmurer" is to disenfranchise harmony, disassociates themselves from hope, and discombobulates those who are willing to help. The intent of the murmurer is to defy God's order for an accomplishment, and persuade as many others as they possibly can to do the same. We will find ways on how to handle the "order violator" later in our text.

You place yourself on the line when you tell people what they need to hear rather than what they want to hear.

A Violation of Order Is Manifested When It Seeks To Usurp Leadership

One of the dangers of trying to get people who are out of order to get in some order is there are times when they will blame you, the leader, for the past situation, the present situation and even your suggestion for future resolve. If there has been an issue that has been silenced, swept under the rug, not acknowleged or not addressed for quite some time, and a leader shows up to address it or bring some attention to it, it should not be a surprise if attack is soon to follow. When the murmurers did not want to possess the land, they surfaced and sought to remove Moses from his pastoral responsibilities. It is one thing when people who defy order do not desire for you to lead them, but it is another thing when erroneous, divisive, unethical and ungodly attack occurs in the attempt to unseat the leader who is sent to establish order. Ronald Heifitz and Martin Linsky gave validity to the idea when they stated "You appear dangerous to people when you question their values, beliefs, or habits of a lifetime. You place yourself on the line when you tell people what they need to hear rather than what they want to hear. Although you may see it with clarity and passion a promising future of progress and gain, people will see with equal passions the losses you are asking them to sustain." (Walter Earl Fluker, *Ethical Leadership-The Quest for Character, Civility, and Community*, Fortress Press, Minneapolis, p. p.8).

And they said one to another, *Let us make a captain, and let us return into Egypt.* The obvious difference between the call of Moses to leadership and the call of the congregations' captain is, Moses was appointed by God and the congregations' captain was appointed by themselves. If you are going to serve in leadership while "doing church," it is most important you position yourself not to be the object of the issue being denied or protested against. For example, imagine a church where the pastor may have a vision to do outreach in a community infested with the sale of drugs, riffed with gun and gang violence, the hot spot for police calls and ambulatory presence, yet there is a delegation in the church that may rise in protest and issue a vote against the pastor because they refuse or don't have the desire to deal with the real issue of community decay around them. The issue for the pastor is the community; the issue for this church is the pastor. In my own pastoral experience with the conflict I mentioned earlier, the issue for me was the misuse of power and financial account-ability, but the delegation that sought to usurp my leadership made "me" the issue. While the group will make you the issue, you can't make you the issue. "When you take 'personal' attacks personally, you unwittingly conspire in one of the common ways you can be taken out of action-you make yourself the issue." (Ronald A. Heifetz and Marty Linsky, Leadership On The Line: Staying Alive Through the Dangers of Leading, Harvard Business School Press, Boston, Mass., p. 191). The action is the issue you want to address, and a good leader knows how to keep it on the issue, and not make it about themselves. This is what Moses did because when Moses goes to God, he becomes an intercessor for the people who are seeking to stone him. *19 Pardon, I beseech thee, the iniquity of this people according unto the greatness of thy mercy, and as thou hast forgiven this people, from Egypt even until now.*

I believe a real measurement for whether one is walking in mature leadership or not, is the leader's ability to rise above chaos, confusion, and calamity.

I believe a real measurement for whether one is walking in mature leadership or not, is the leader's ability to rise above chaos, confusion, and calamity, and still perform the ministerial task for which they have been called to. Do not make the attack personal. This is not about you, this is about the will of God, and the place where God is trying to take his church. In the game of football, when the defensive line is viciously seeking to hit a swift running back, the running back can't take the hit personal. The running back has the ball, and he must understand part of the penalty for carrying the ball is every now and then he will get hit. It's not personal; it's just the way the game is played. This is the mindset you must have, because you as the leader carry the ball, and there are times when the game will require you to be hit.

Whenever there is the lack of order in any church, more often than not, the problem can always be traced back to some issue/s around integrity.

If you as a leader ever have to face this kind of conflict in your ministry, it is important to hold on to some essential qualities as leaders that will aid you in your authority. Order is often maintained when the leader maintains three qualities in particular: Integrity, Empathy, and Hope, as cited in Ethical Leadership by Walter Fluka.

The Leader With Integrity

The Chinese symbol for integrity is *Te*. While this could also mean virtue and goodness, the best interpretation for this is character comes straight from the heart. (Walter Earl Fluker, *Ethical Leadership-The Quest for Character, Civility, and Community*, Fortress Press, Minneapolis, p. 66). Thus integrity is that which comes straight from the heart. The leader's integrity is important because it informs actions and behaviors. Whenever there is the lack of order in any church, more often than not, the problem can always be traced back to some issue/s around integrity. People who come up with schemes in the church, plan deceptive forms of operation, circulate gossip, disrupt meetings, and intentionally mislead others suffer from a spiritual sickness. At the root of their actions are also an issue of integrity. For the leader integrity must be practiced in what the leaders says, does, and how he or she behaves. Integrity must inform the leaders choices, guide direction, and serve as a thermometer for emotions.

Howard G. Hendricks reminded leaders on the importance of integrity when he stated Vision without integrity is not mission- it's manipulation. (Roy B. Zuck, *The Speaker's Quote Book*, Kregal Publications 1997, Grand Rapids, Michigan, p. 212) It is most important to note integrity and character must become the foundation and basis for effectiveness in ministry.

It is interesting to me the adversaries of Moses attacked his vision, but never accused him of living a life void of integrity. If there had been an integrity issue with Moses like infidelity, embezzlement, lying, cheating, and stealing, then these issues would have taken precedence over their fear for possessing the promise land. In other words, the issue of integrity would have served as a smoke screen to cover the real issue of fear to possess the promise land. While no one is perfect, perfection as a leader must be your aim. You will make errors while leading, but let it be an error made while trying to make the kingdom better, rather than an error made for self-indulging and manipulative means for private gain. Lord Macauley declared, "The measure a man's character is what he would do if he knew he would never be found out." "Character is what you are in the dark, and reputation is only what others believe you to be." (Vernon McLellan, Timeless Treasures, Hendrickson Publishers, Peabody, Massachusetts, 1992, 2000, p.33). Moses did not allow his integrity to slip into a place he wasn't familiar with, Moses reverted to prayer. The integrity of Moses led him to not only pray for himself, but to pray for his murmurers. This has to be foundational for the leader, and that is you can't lead them if you hate them.

The Leader with Empathy

While integrity is more about behavior, empathy is more about emotions. The reason the leader must possess empathy particularly while addressing issues concerning order in the church is because empathy has a way of helping the leader to put themselves in the place of the people who may be expressing disgust, and the lack of cooperation. Moses must have had empathy for the people, because it is out of his empathy he begins to pray for God to spare their lives. Empathy has a way of hearing a person's story differently, and understand in some way why they may refuse to receive the newness God has to offer, but rather choose to hold on to the past.

There must be a balance between what you empathize with, and what you know you are assigned to correct and direct.

While it is important for the leader to have empathy, the leader must be ever cautious of not negotiating what God has commissioned over what they are feeling. In other words, the leader's empathy is not an excuse for not executing the assignment God has already given. In other words, Pastor/Leader listen to the congregations' stories, hear how passionate they are about their past, enter into the world of the sensitive, and the things that mean something to them. But while you are empathizing with their history, or their desire, it is incumbent you always return to your world of what God commissioned you do. 2 Timothy 4:2-4 says, "Preach the word; be instant in season, out of season; reprove, rebuke, exhort with all longsuffering and doctrine. For the time will come when they will not endure sound doctrine; but after their own lusts shall they heap to themselves teachers, having itching ears; 4 And they shall turn away *their* ears from the truth, and shall be turned unto fables." This is what Jesus did with the woman who was caught in adultery. His empathy led him to dismiss her charge and not stone or judge her, but his divine commission to her was for her to go and sin no more. There must be a balance between what you empathize with, and what you know you are assigned to correct and direct.

The Leader with Hope

Nothing can hinder your creativity and diminish your optimism like people in the church who refuse to follow proper protocol and do things the right way. Nothing can affect the flow of peace and unity like a disgruntled "church doer" who only desires for things to be done their way, and no other way. Nothing can disturb the sacredness of church work like someone who does not have a healthy perception of themselves, and has to depend on their title to make them important and significant. However, even though there are times when the leader will encounter these challenges, it is important for the leader to always exemplify a ray of hope. James Gustafon describes hope as confidence in our future. He stated, "Hope is carried by confidence that life is more reliable than unreliable, that the future is open, that new possibilities of life exist" (James M. Gustafon, *Christ and the Moral Life*, Chicago and London: Chicago University Press, 1968, p.250) This must be the reality every leader must hold on to if that leader is serious about leading people who do not have hope. The leader must be serious about confronting the despair disgruntled people bring, with the Hope that leaders have a right to anticipate. Hope is not just being optimistic, or having a positive outlook on the situation, but hope is rooted in the faith that says even when things don't look quite optimistic, we can still have hope. Hebrews 11:1 says, "Now faith is the substance of things hoped for, the evidence of things not seen." Before any

"Hope is carried by confidence that life is more reliable than unreliable, that the future is open, that new possibilities of life exist."

There are countless occasions where leaders have served for years, and ended up holding an empty bag.

radical transformation is to happen in the lives of people who resist change, they must be empowered by hope. The pastor/leader must make them feel like if we lose everything in our attempt to get to the Canaan land, we will still have our hope.

The Leader with Security

It is vital for any leader seeking to implement a vision, to be certain about where their security lies. The security for the leader cannot be in the succession of leadership, or in the success of the person you have followed. Security is not necessarily in how many years you have served, or in how much you have invested. There are countless occasions where leaders have served for years, and ended up holding an empty bag. Nor is our security found in the people who serve on our security ministries, or those who sense they have a call to protect you. Therefore, the security of your position has to solely be in God, and not in any governing board, denominational discipline, or any man or woman. It is God who will plant you, and it is God who will keep you.

This is so apparent in Moses' experience. Because even though the Israelites decided to defy order, God did not. The Israelites desired to select another leader, which it seems that this move would have threatened Moses' security. But Moses did not have his security in them, his security was in God. Even when they wanted to defy order, God never seconded their motion. I know that because in Numbers 14:4, they elected another leader. But in verse 11 it is evidence God never pays attention to their selection, because this verse clearly shows God still spoke to Moses. In other words, God's order will never be secondary to humankind's order. What I am trying to convey is that when God establishes you as a leader, and ordains you to a place, your security has to rest in the fact it is God who ordered you to be there. Though there are times when murmurers can change their plans, they can never change God's order. If by chance human will and human manipulation would lead a group to get rid of you, or remove you from your leadership post, just remember God will provide and take care of you and the ministry He has placed within you. I once heard a notable preacher say, "It is my job to jump, and it is God's job to find me a place to land." This is the security of the leader. Therefore, your leadership must possess confidence, optimism, drive, and zeal. You can have these attributes when you learn where to put your trust. God has not called you to lead in fear, looking over your shoulder or whether or not you will be the order of the day at the next church conference. You must lead while trusting God, Isaiah 54:4a "Fear not; for thou shalt not be ashamed: neither be thou confounded; for thou shalt not be put to shame..."

Practical Tips For Leaders Under Attack

1. It is important for the leader to understand disgruntled members love to have meetings. Look out for this request, and be open for meeting when you feel it is the right time. In this meeting spend time gathering information and discerning the root of the problem.

2. When the meeting is called, it is important for you establish the location. Do not fall into the temptation of meeting on their territory for this is certainly not "holy ground." Make certain the meeting is either in your office, in your place of choosing, most preferably at the church. Try to avoid lunches, walks in the park, or golfing adventures with people who are disgruntled. This creates an environment of friendliness that may compromise discussing the real issue at hand.

3. When the leader is meeting with a disgruntled member, there are times when having a witness with you is helpful. We are living in a day where fallacies are used to oust a leader, and if your spirit leads you to have a witness by all means do so. If a witness is not available, if possible leave the door open, or have someone close by if you fear physical harm. Also note there are times when a witness will elevate to the matter and make the issue more important than it really is.

4. Avoid keeping secrets. If there is any information a disgruntled member would like for you to share with them, always let them know that you will be willing to share it with a committee or the entire church body if necessary. You are accountable to the church, not one disgruntled member.

5. When meeting a disgruntled member always be mindful of your Christian posture, but remain firm. Make certain you arrive before time, because disgruntled members often arrive early as they can't wait to get the issue off of their chest. In the meeting let them talk first, and do not affirm what they are saying with either a yes or a no. You will have your chance, just listen. Take good notes as a record, and use the time they are talking as a gathering moment for you to organize your talking points.

6. When responding to a disgruntled member, keep your answers short and your words very selective. Remember even though they are not writing doesn't mean they aren't taking notes, or either "secretly" recording the conversation. Never say anything to a disgruntled member you can't repeat in open court. In your mind, you should always anticipate the matter can get to that level, and if it does you want to be able to repeat whatever is said.

7. If a disgruntled member desires for you to maintain confidentiality, you must remember to do so if it is a personal matter. However, if what they are discussing is a church matter, it automatically becomes a public issue. This is where you draw the line with confidentiality. You are accountable to the church, and therefore, are obligated to inform the church on matters that are critical and important.

8. When addressing disgruntled members always expect the unexpected. Do not let anything surprise, but learn to anticipate the worst action. If it happens simply learn to say, "I knew you would do this, so God and I are well prepared."

CHAPTER 5

CREATIVE CHURCH IS PRECEDED BY ORDER

While it is important to note the Israelites were out of order when they sought to defy the plan of God, the truth of the matter is that this reality happens often as we seek to "do church." It is imperative the body of Christ recognizes what God wants from the church today is for the church to be in order, because when you study the government of the demonic, the rule and the reign of the satanic, you will find that they are organized, systematic and on assignment to do just what John 10:10 says, "The thief cometh not, but for to steal, and to kill, and to destroy....." Ephesians 6:12 reveals the order of the satanic, when it says [12] For we wrestle not against flesh[b] and blood, but against principalities, against powers, against the rulers of the darkness of this world, against spiritual wickedness in high *places*." Principalities comes from the Greek word *arche*, which means demonic establishment executive authority or governmental rule. *Arche* is where we get the word archive from. These demonic influences are keepers of the old, traditionalism, and religious routine that seek more to please religious establishment than they do God. Powers comes from the Greek word *exousia*, which are demonic forces that have been given the right to execute the plan of the principalities. The Powers are responsible for inspiring corrupt church practices, deceit upon deacons, and trickery among trustees. Some attribute the work of drug cartels, gross poverty, plagues, terrorism, and other heinous crimes against humanity to this level of spiritual operation. <u>Rulers of Darkness</u> are the armed forces of the demonic, and they come with spiritual wickedness. <u>Spiritual wickedness</u> comes from the Greek word *poneros*, which means to antagonize or to cause a malicious act in the way of witchcraft. Witchcraft is control and manipulation, and it comes from the Greek word, *python*, and a python is a snake the squeezes the life out of living organisms. Therefore, spiritual wickedness is about controlling and manipulating the church by destroying the life of the church.

Spiritual wickedness is about controlling and manipulating the church by destroying the life of the church.

So in the kingdom of the demonic there is order. Their order is established to cause disorder in the church and in your life. If there is order in the government of the satanic, then there must be order in church. I Corinthian 14:40 declares, "But all things should be done decently and in order." However, before we seek to illustrate ways to establish order, it is essential we consider ways order is defied in the church among leaders, officers, volunteers, and laity.

When Clergy Are Out of Order

- Clergy are out of order when their ministry is centered around destroying with their tongue and tactics other ministries and not focusing on the development of their own ministry.

- Clergy are out of order when they participate in the destruction of other Bishops, Elders, Pastors, and clergy. All clergy are on the

---

[b] flesh...: Gr. blood and flesh

same team. If you don't always agree on methods of ministry, this does not mean you have a right to destroy other clergy. "What goes around comes around."

- Clergy are out of order when the pulpit is used to preach their insecurities and their personal hang-ups, and not center on the hope that is found in Christ. The pulpit should be used to pull people out of their pit, and then turn around and put them back in a pit.

- Clergy are out of order when they get to the point in their preaching they only get happy off of their own preaching. There is something to learn from every sermon even a bad one. If you hear a bad sermon you just can't get happy off of, get happy every time they mention a book in the Bible you are familiar with. Find something to affirm.

- Clergy are out of order when relationships are developed with the members that can hinder their ability to minister truthfully and accurately the integrity that is found in Christian living. Always remember, whoever you sin with, has the potential of sinning against you.

- Clergy are out of order when their human desires and out of the pulpit lifestyles are such that shame is brought to the church and the body of Christ. Clergy should always be mindful of their image, and the representation of their ministry. A good measure for this is to raise this question, "Can I explain what I am doing, if by chance I get caught." If you can't explain it without shame, you might not need to engage in it.

- Clergy are out of order when they elevate themselves with titles they did not earn. It is a violation of a spiritual law to make yourself an apostle, a bishop, a "doctor" or even a prophet or prophetess. While these are legitimate titles for ministry, these titles must be affirmed by a representing body of faith that can witness the evidence of these titles, and can share in the validity of you becoming and receiving this title placed upon your name. Know that Lord did not say He will make your title great, God said He will make your name great. You have a great name without a title.

When Associate Ministers Are Out Of Order

- Associate Ministers are out of order when they solicit or invite themselves to preach in a pulpit. There is a difference in being ready to preach at all times, and presenting yourself as a salesperson of your gift. Just be faithful and available and your gift will make room for you.

- Associate Ministers are out of order when they say, "I know what's on the program, but the Lord told me to say this....and that." If you did not get permission from the pastor to alter any part of that program, the minister is out of order. If the Lord told you, the Lord will also confirm this with the pastor; therefore, get permission from the pastor first.

- Associate Ministers are out of order when they visit the hospital on behalf of the pastor and the church, and never mentioned they are there on behalf of the pastor and the church, which allows the minister to get the credit for visiting and not the corporate ministry.

- Associate Ministers are out of order when they leave a ministry to start a ministry without having a conversation or dialogue with the pastor they are presently serving under. Leaving without getting the blessing of that ministry can be detrimental to the future of the new-found ministry. Therefore, do all you can to communicate your move, and by all means do not seek to build your ministry with members where you presently serve.

- Associate Ministers are out of order when they pray or read Scripture longer than the preacher preaches. Always be mindful of the fact there is power in brevity, and it doesn't take a long time to do anything for the ministry to be blessed.

- Associate Ministers must always do what you are asked to do. If you are asked to pray, that does not mean read a Scripture or sing a song first and then pray. The request was to pray. Obedience is better than sacrifice. If you are asked to read Scripture, it does not mean the entire chapter, it simply means the relevant periscope unless otherwise printed or stated. Use common judgment when leading a congregation in worship.

- Associate Ministers, when leading worship, must be mindful of the difference between worship leading and preaching. It is inappropriate to slip in a sermon because the choir has the congregation motivated. Your job is to be like John the Baptist, you are to simply prepare the way for the designated preacher. Not too many churches can handle two preachers "hooping" in the same service.

When Officers Are Out of Order

- Officers are out of order when they expect to perform their duties and responsibilities without the passion for Christian study and biblical understanding.

- Officers are out of order when they place secular rules and regulations over the establishment of God's word for governing the ministry.

- Officers are out of order when they see their position as autonomous, and negate to realize their position exists for the good of the church, and not their personal agenda.

- Officers are out of order when they believe what they do in their secular job, qualifies them for spiritual task. Just because you are an accountant, doesn't mean your spirit is right to count church money.

- Officers are out of order when they have a place during worship on the front row, but use the front row to sleep, murmur, or satisfy their need for importance. If you are on the front row, you should catch on fire before the worshipers on the back row.

- Officers are out of order when a vision is set for the ministry, and they refuse to show physical or financial support for the effort the church has chosen to embrace.

- Officers are out of order when they foster ill spirit among the congregation, and foster division among the members about operations or pertinent church matters. The proper time to convey this information is during formal meeting times and organized church settings when the matter can be addressed in order at the proper time.

- Officers are out of order when they confer issues that they are not happy about to the Court of Law. While there are some operations in ministry that may require legal guidance, referring church issues to the Court of Law is not the best policy for handling God's business. Do all you can to reason out the matter, and seek peace in all of your ways.

- Officers are out of order when they collect the tithe, but don't leave a tithe. Worst than that, steal the tithe.

When Choirs and Praise Teams Are Out of Order

- Choirs and Praise Team are out of order when they do not possess a spirit of worship, and do not have an attitude that is representative of the church and the Holy Spirit.

- Choirs and Praise Teams are out of order when they only show in worship or participate in worship when it is their time to perform. Choirs and Praise Teams must show reverence for worship and not just performance.

- Choirs and Praise Teams are out of order when they seek to lift their singing ability over other ministries in the church. Just because their position is highly visible, does not mean their ministry is more significant than another. The church is one body, with many parts.

- Choirs and Praise Teams are out of order when they are out of dress code. If the dress code is black and silver, that means the choir member that shows up in black, silver, and orange is out of order. It is important order is represented in the decorum which has a way of strengthening unity.

- Choirs and Praise Teams are out of order when they mount the choir stand late, or begin the worship late. God deserves our best effort, and it does not speak well of excellence to be late. If you are late, there should be an appointed time for late members to mount the choir stand, certainly not in the middle of a song or if the choir is already singing.

- Choirs and Praise teams are out of order when they cannot adapt to the change of the Holy Spirit in worship services. Just because you rehearse a song, and the song is printed on the program does not mean it must be sung. The Holy Spirit may direct the worship in another direction, the choir and praise team must be open to the move of the Spirit. "I didn't get to sing my song." Technically, it is not your song; the song belongs to the artist who recorded it. If you don't own the copyrights, it's not "your song."

When Ushers Are Out of Order

- Ushers are out of order when they do not visibly show a spirit of hospitality while performing their responsibilities. If there is any ministry that should demonstrate the fruit of the spirit, the ushers should possess it.

- Ushers are out of order when they are out of dress code, and do not exemplify order with the uniformity of the dress attire when necessary.

- Ushers are out of order when they point people to their seating, and not take the time to lead them.
- Ushers are out of order when the church is filled to capacity, and they are sitting while there are guests standing.
- Ushers are out of order when they are not paying attention to directives from the pulpit, or the adjustments that need to be made in the worship service.
- Ushers are out of order when they constrain people who are shouting, aggressively shake people who are slain in the spirit, and do not keep emergency matters at a level of calm.
- Ushers are out of order when they walk, talk, or pass out programs during the time of praying, Scripture reading, and especially during the preaching moment.
- Ushers are out of order when they get to church late, and leave before benediction. The usher should be one of the last one's out of the church. It will be helpful to check the pews for paper, gum, and any obvious trash before leaving the sanctuary.
- Ushers are out of order when they lead the tithe but don't leave a tithe.

When Staff Workers Are Out of Order

- Staff workers are out of order when they deliberately violate the confidentiality of church business affairs, or concerns of the membership.
- Staff workers are out of order when they manipulate their staff position to possess power and control over the membership who pay their salary.
- Staff workers are out of order when the take the ministry for granted, do not provide adequate reporting, come to work late, do not offer their best work, and give the church less than a high level of excellency.

- Staff workers are out of order whenever they rebel against a directive from the pastor, and show any form of disrespect towards the position of the pastor or any member of the first family.
- Staff workers are out of order when they discuss the travel schedule of the pastor or share private information concerning the pastor or the pastor's family with anybody inside or outside of the church.
- Staff workers are out of order when they develop 'cliques" with the members, and develop secret relationships that can compromise their integrity to function as a staff member of the church.
- Staff workers are out of order when they join a contentious group that may be against the vision or the direction for which the church desires to move in.
- Staff workers are out of order when they get paid from the tithe, but won't leave a tithe.

When Volunteers (Sound and Video Technicians, Parking Attendants, Security, Kitchen Workers, Van Drivers, and Other Volunteer Ministries) Are Out of Order

- Volunteers are out of order when they do not have the highest respect, honor, and regard for God with their service.
- Volunteers are out of order when they arrive late to provide their service. Volunteers are still expected to be on time.
- Volunteers are out of order when they do not have a spirit of hospitality, and serve with an attitude that is not pleasing to God.
- Volunteers are out of order when they make a commitment to serve or lead a committee and do not follow through on their commitment and refuse to follow directives that are given to them.
- Volunteers are out of order when they do not understand their volunteerism is under the direction of pastoral leadership, official boards, paid staff, and those who are appointed to serve over them.

- Volunteers are out of order when they do not take the time to study God's word, learn their area of service, and stay in their lane when providing their service.
- Volunteers are out of order when they find areas of improvement in the ministry, and openly discuss their frustrations among the other congregants and visitors.

When the Congregation Is Out of Order

- The congregation is out of order when they do not submit to the leadership of God, and the vision God desires for their church.
- The congregation is out of order when respect is not given to the pastor at all times, and honor is not extended with highest respect for the office.
- The congregation is out of order when they openly rebel with malice, vengeance, contriteness, and a spirit to do their own will and not the Lord's will.
- The congregation is out of order when they come to church late, do not participate in the worship, do not adhere to the directives of the worship leader, don't touch their "neighbor" when asked, and see church is an option and not a necessity.
- The congregation is out of order when they do not financially support the church, but benefit from its services and the benefits it has to offer.
- The congregation is out of order when they do not come to Bible study, pay their tithes, give their time, and offer their talent to be used for the glory of God.
- The congregation is out of order when members are not mindful of their hygiene in worship. While there are some who have no option about securing good hygiene before coming to church, for the most part, good physical stewardship is making certain that

you bathe, brush your teeth, put on deodorant, and for breath freshness - a piece of mint in your pocket.

- The congregation is out of order when they don't attend Bible study, but will show up for church meetings to cause confusion over issues they don't agree with.
- The congregation is out of order when they do not put their faith in God to bring the vision, ministry efforts, and the resources that are needed for the church to be effective.

STEPS FOR IMPLEMENTING ORDER IN THE CHURCH

Organization Is the key to Order and Vision Implementation

One of the greatest atrocities that pastors/ leaders make as it pertains to vision implementation is to believe vision is implemented automatically. The implementation of vision not only requires an announcement there is a vision, but vision requires organization and a plan for putting the vision in place. C. Peter Wagner, researcher and statistician for the church culture, observed that only five percent of pastors ever come up with new ideas, concepts, or observations. Another 15 percent of pastors are what he calls, "innovators," which means they are innovative enough to follow the template of ideas demonstrated by the five percent who create great ideas in ministry. This means 80% of pastors are what Wagner calls "programmatic," which means this group rarely comes up with any-thing new to do in ministry. As a matter of fact, if

One of the greatest atrocities that pastors/leaders make as it pertains to vision implementation is to believe vision is implemented automatically.

something is suggested, they need very detailed steps to actually imple-ment what has been placed before them. (7 Steps To Transform Your Church, Baker Book House, Grand Rapids, MI, 1997, Bill Hull, p.39).

Regardless of where you find yourself in Wagner's research, it is important as a leader you get organized. The lack of order is often caused by the lack of organization on the part of the pastor/leader. Therefore, to mobilize any group of people to accomplish a task, it is momentous the vision be made clear. For a pastor who is trying to accomplish a vision, it may be helpful to write the vision, and make it plain. Writing the vision today can be done by writing on an old fashion chalk board, or with tech-nology like power point, internet technology, architectural three dimen-sional designs, or a phone tree system that can communicate with your members while they are in their home. Some churches are even making good use of text messaging and emailing to communicate ministry ideas and opportunities.

One of the greatest attributes for my ministry has been using one Sunday out of the year to have what I call, "The State of the Church Address." During Sunday morning worship in the month of January, I will present the vision of the ministry for that year to the church. This is a power point presentation, with all of the church leaders sitting in a body. During this worship I will review our performance as a church from the previous year, and then unfold vision and goals for the new year. There are four categories that are discussed; worship, Christian education, evan-gelism, finances, and physical development. Each category should have very clear and defined goals. The power point should encompass a picture that will enhance what you are introducing. Once you introduce these ministry goals for the year, you must then organize committees, volun-teers, and staff to make certain they come to pass. My advice to any pastor or leader is if you are not a good organizer, get people around you who are. Because once you announce the vision and goal to the church, you are also responsible for making certain it comes to pass.

This practice has been very effective for me, because it keeps me praying for fresh vision. It also shapes my drive for the year to make certain that what is announced to the congregation actually becomes a reality. Don't forget, you have to explain the next January on why it did or did not come to pass. What a system of accountability!

Organization involves writing the vision, researching the feasibility, knowing the pros and cons of the ministry idea.

Organization involves writing the vision, researching the feasibility, knowing the pros and cons of the ministry idea, having a knowledge base of the resources that will be needed to make it happen, gathering the people who will assist in the ministry implementation, establishing benchmarks, budgeting, networking, and remaining steadfast until it happens. Most of the time, if the organization is there, the order is there. This is not to say the order will not be tested, but with organization the areas of question are much easier to address.

<u>Re</u>-Design Ministry Focus with Information

Most of the time whenever a pastor or leader is confronted with opposition it happens because there is a need to make some changes. If you are seeking to re-design a concept of ministry, it is important you make changes with information. The primary source of information for any ministry re-design should be the authority that is presented in the Scriptures. When presenting a new direction, or the need for ministry opportunity, show where the vision or the idea is theological, biblical, and has good grounding with God. For example, our church just purchased an ice cream truck to aide our efforts in doing evangelism. An ice cream truck is not in the Bible, but reaching the lost is the fundamental purpose for Jesus coming. So in presenting the ministry idea, I focused on evangelism, not the ice cream truck. Today we have the gospel ice cream truck in operation, and we have numbers to show we were able to put ministry tracks in the hands of thousands as a result. While sharing Christ, the truck drives around the community with a big sign that says, "Our Ice Cream is Blessed and Highly Flavored." This slogan is reflected on the truck along with the advertisement of praise pops, blessed nutty buddies, comfort chocolate, and sanctified strawberry ice cream sandwiches.

Information is not only found biblically, but books and internet research has been proven to be extremely helpful. Also exposure is another form of gathering information.

If you are seeking to introduce your church to new ways of "doing church," exposure for information is a major benefactor. There are times when sharing the vision or ministry idea via technology is not enough. There are times when an actual site of what is desired is the best example. This form of gathering information is demonstrated by tours to various churches, locations or sites where what you desire as a leader is already established. For example, if there is a certain style of church you have a vision about leading your church into building, it will be most helpful if you would find churches that exist in that style, and take your leaders there. While this may cost you financially, look at it as an investment. Once the delegation actually witness what you have been visioning, their excitement can help convince others this is the move the ministry needs to make.

Gathering information requires you putting aside your hang ups about denomination, mega church –vs- small church, whether it is a white church, black church or Latino church, in town or out of town. These factors are not important. What is important is that if it exists then you want to see it.

Once this information is gathered how it is presented is also important. Regardless of how you choose to present the information, make certain there is order in the presentation.

Direct the What You Expect

Directing a ministry plan involves preaching, teaching, demonstrating, and explaining what you as a leader expect every opportunity you get. Expectation is not mentioned in the way of being dictatorial, but expectation in the sense of raising a standard. Directing a ministry plan involves delegation. If a vision is to be implemented with order, you must be secure enough to delegate responsibility, and have a system in place to evaluate its effectiveness. A vision is not effective if it only remains with you. However, you can't carry the burden of the vision alone. Directing what you expect is not necessarily the leader doing the actual work, but the leader serves somewhat in the capacity of a coach, or one who has the responsibility of planning, equipping, motivating, and then letting the players play the game. If a leader does not learn to delegate, it is possible "burn out," a point of exhaustion mentally, emotionally, spiritually, and physically, can soon become a significant matter.

The Fuller Theological Seminary did a study on the stress and strain that goes along with pastoring and leading a church. Consider the following statistics that will reveal the pastors need for delegating authority.

- 90 percent of pastors work more than 46 hours per week.
- 80 percent believe pastoral ministry is affecting their families negatively.
- 33 percent say "Being in ministry is clearly a hazard to my family."
- 75 percent have reported a significant crisis due to stress at least once in their ministry.
- 50 percent felt unable to meet the needs of the ministry.

- 90 percent felt they were not adequately trained to cope with the ministry demands placed upon them.
- 40 percent reported at least one serious conflict with at least one parishioner at least once a month.
- 70 percent of pastors do not have someone they would consider a close friend.
- 37 percent admitted having been involved in inappropriate sexual behaviors with someone in their congregation
- 70 percent have a lower self-image after they have been in pastoral ministry that when they started (Fred Lehr, *Clergy Burnout*, Fortress Press, Minneapolis, p.4.)

These statistics reflect the stress and strain that comes with doing church. Because the work is demanding and stressful, it is imperative as a leader you learn to delegate responsibilities to who you can trust, and who is loyal and able.

Directing what you expect takes risk and patience. In the end the hope is not to have the aforementioned numbers become a reality. If order is to be maintained in the church, it begins with the leader who is well rested and has the health needed to lead people in "doing church."

"Excellence is not a skill, but it's an attitude." It is this mindset that makes excellence in ministry achievable for any ministry.

Elevate Expectation with Ministry Excellence

Implementing a creative vision that has the potential of being threatened by people who murmur must never be negotiated for the necessity of excellence. To elevate any ministry to a higher standard of operation. The goal should be to first interpret for the members what excellence means to you because it is possible their expectation of excellence, and your expectation of excellence, can be quite different. One wise writer declared, "Excellence is not a skill, but it's an attitude." It is this mindset that makes excellence in ministry achievable for any ministry. If you are in ministry where the mindset is to just do enough to get by, or the very minimum will do, remember excellence is an attitude. So if a ministry is accustomed to grass not being manicured, the steeple leaning to the side on top of the church, the restrooms having a stench, and the pulpit is cluttered with programs from previous services, there has to be a way to elevate the expectancy for excellence. Consider a few suggestions:

1. Make certain the people for which you lead clearly understand the expectation God has for the church as you interpret it. While interpreting God's expectation, you also express your expectancy for your ministry staff, your ministry leaders, your volunteers who participate in ministry. Clear expectations can alleviate the lack of order later.

2. Know excellence begins with the leader. Therefore, as a leader it is good for your members to know you refuse to settle for less than best. As a leader it is critical you be on time as much as possible, when you show up, you should show up with a plan and evidence of preparation. Always be mindful of your appearance and show confidence in what it is God has called you to do. Excellence has to be demonstrated by you, and be synonymous with your name and title.

3. Excellence requires communication and training. There are times when you as a leader must invest in the people you expect to demonstrate excellence. This intimate time with your leaders at retreats, picnics, golfing tournaments, or breakfast in the fellowship hall, is critical for your leaders understanding your level of expectancy. You will discover some major things that are happening in the ministry can be handled with some very minor discussions.

Often times it is not that people desire to be out of order, you have to take the time to tell them how critical it is to be in order. Spend quality time, and quality results will follow.

4. Excellence requires commitment of time, talent, and treasurer. One of the things I seek to do while building a ministry concept with a committee is allow them to vision without a budget. Often times if you place a budget on a ministry vision, your vision may come out looking like your budget. There is a time when budget comes in to play, but let's get the vision out first, then discuss what is affordable and what is not affordable. The Leader should aim high, because the people you are leading will often be the ones who will aim low. But never negate the fact God sent you to elevate the expectation of excellence.

Reclaiming Relationships are Critical for Ministry Transformation

To speak of reclaiming relationships, is to say making relationships the primary reason for "doing church" in the first place. I have discovered most of the time people do things that are out of order in the church, weather it is showing up in a different color from the rest of the choir, acting unbecomingly in a church meeting, not supporting a ministry goal that is set, because of a need for connection and relationship.

When people are isolated they have the tendency not to act or think corporately. Therefore, putting emphasis on relationships in any ministry can be very beneficial for order and ministry success. While leading you are going to lose some relationships, and you are going to gain some. The challenge is finding your priority for relationship in the midst of this.

Relationships are essential if you are going to lead any ministry in transformation. Whenever a leader begins to feel they can function on their own, this can lead to what Heifetz and Linskey call "Heroic Suicide." "Relating to people is central to leading and staying alive. If you are not naturally a political person, then find partners who have that ability to be intensely conscious of the importance of relationships in getting challenging work done...Let them (allies) help you relate to your opposition, those people who feel that they have the most to lose in your initiative." ((Ronald A. Heifetz and Marty Linsky, *Leadership On The Line: Staying Alive Through the Dangers of Leading*, Harvard Business School Press, Boston, Mass.p.100)

Reclaiming relationships also speaks to leaving the ninety-nine and seeking the one lost sheep. In any transition there will be casualties or people who will just drop out of the game. As a Christian leader do your part in establishing relationships, but in the end, know it is the choice of every individual to either accept your attempt or reject it. Just make certain you make the attempt to reconcile matters that are critical for transformation.

PREACHING THAT SHAPES CREATIVE MINISTRY

How do we preach to people who live in a world of fast transition, high market systems and intimidating technology? What do you say to people who work countless hours a week, being dutiful to the philosophy of a company, but have to watch jobs be sent to other countries as if loyalty means nothing? What do you preach to people who have to live in a place where governmental and political systems continue to fail them, and the value of the dollar continues to decrease while the prices of gas, electricity, rent, and mortgage continues to increase? What do you say to people who are living with the threat of terrorism and war staring them in their face, while at the same time they already have to live in neighborhoods that are ravaged with violence, community crime, health ills, noise nuisance, and the threat of police brutality? What do you say to people who live in a world where morals have taken a nose-dive into the abyss of shame and wickedness, where evil is running rampant, peril and sword seems to be a natural way? What do you say to people whose families are being hijacked by illicit and immoral practices, and in these times where our children are turning to dope for hope, crime that's got them doing time, illicit sexual practices for the validation of their identities and their sexual selves? There should be something we as people of faith can

Preaching to shape creative and innovative ministry is an essential component to proclamation of God's word, and it's capacity to ignite action and creativity.

say that would give some direction to people who are in desperate need for an answer. To address these matters through the preaching of the gospel, there must be a convincing that preaching is still relevant and still works.

Preaching to shape creative and innovative ministry is an essential component to proclamation of God's word, and its capacity to ignite action and creativity has undisputed evidence. The New Testament makes reference to preaching in four different expressions. 1) Evaggelizo- means to share good news. This is the very word that evangel, evangelist, and to evangelize is derived from. This expression can be found in Matthew 11:5, Luke 4:18, I Corinthians 1:17, Hebrews 4:2. 2) Kerusso- means to proclaim herald. This reference to a more public proclamation, as in a church setting when sharing the gospel. You may find reference to this kind of preaching in Matthew 11:1, Mark 1:4, Romans 10:14. 3) Katangello- means to tell in detail which is cited in Acts 4:2, Acts 13:38 and Colossians 1:28. 4) Laleo - means to simply talk as in Mark 2:2 and Acts 14:25. Collectively, to preach means to share good news, to herald the gospel, to explain in great detail, and to simply talk about God and the life, death, resurrection and return of our Christ. Wayne McDill says, "Christian preaching is an expression of the revelation of God through oral communication, declared by a God-called messenger, by the enabling of the Holy Spirit, containing a theological message from a biblical text, addressed to a particular audience in their situation, with the aim of calling the hearers to faith in God"- (*Preaching that Pleases God*, Tom Farrell, p. 11). He goes on to further suggest most preachers admit 90 to 95 percent of preaching seeks to get hearers to do better, while only 5 to 10 percent of preaching is aimed an getting the hearer to enhance their faith. This means most preaching is about moral reform and not simply leading people to see God. In my opinion if preaching gives way for one to see God right, then it invariably leads one to live right.

A.T. Perison declared, "Preaching is a divine act, and therefore the finest of the fine arts. The essence of a sermon is *sermo*-a speech spoken in behalf of, and in the name of a God: in other words, it is in the best sense, a divine oration." Regardless of where you fall in terms of understanding the depth of expression in preaching, what is clear is God has given us the preaching moment to get His word out for people to hear and respond.

The Greek philosopher Aristotle suggested there are three ways in which people hear rhetoric or receive the preacher when he or she stands to preach. Those three formations are ethos (ethics), logos (content), and pathos (passion). To understand the value of what it means to preach as if somebody's life depends on it, I believe that these three components give us keen direction and insight on this perspective of preaching.

Preaching With Ethos

One of the things that allows for one to preach as if somebody's life depends on it, is when their ethics often line up with what they are preaching. There is a marriage between ethics and integrity. The root word of integrity is *integer*. An integer is a whole number numerically that cannot be divided. Therefore, to have integrity means "who" the preacher is, and "what" they are preaching should not reflect a fracture. However, in some instances, the integrity of the preacher has often been challenged around finances, fidelity, flesh, and even faith. The challenge comes because the preacher is human and is susceptible to a human fallen condition we know as sin. Ghandi, the Indian civil rights leader declared sin in such a profound way, when he declared "sin is merely wealth without work, pleasure without conscience, science without humanity, knowledge without character, politics without principle, commerce without morality, worship without sacrifice." Somewhere in this definition of sin, even the preacher will find him or herself. Another described sin as Self-Inflicted-Non-sense. Sin, which seeks to compromise integrity, is not always easily discerned for the preacher. When you consider the Native American approach to killing a wolf it is quite interesting as to how the trapping takes place. The Native Americans had what they called knife traps. One method was to take a knife and stick the handle into a ground, with the blade protruding out of the ground. The hunter would then blanket the blade with blood from venison, and let the blood freeze on the blade. This scheme was done knowing that when the wolf would approach the knife, the wolf would begin licking the frozen blood from their knife. As the heat from the wolf's mouth melts the blood he is licking from the knife, eventually one of the licks would cut his tongue right down the middle, licking the blade.

"Preaching is making a deposit in the hearts and minds of men and women, but also being able to write a check off of the same account."

Unfortunately some people treat sin and temptation the same way, not knowing that what they are devouring without any restraint can eventually lead to their death. Therefore, the preacher must treat integrity as a must for themselves, and not a virtue bestowed by others *We have the treasure in earthen vessels, But we have this treasure in earthen vessels, that the excellency of the power may be of God, and not of us.* 2 Corinthians 4:7

Creative Ministry must be undergirded with the preacher standing as a whole person, and rest assured the substance of what they say is backed up with how they live. One wise writer once declared

"Preaching is making a deposit in the hearts and minds of men and women, but also being able to write a check off of the same account" (*The Four Voices of Preaching*, Brazos Press, Grand, Michigan, Robert Stephen Reid). What the preacher proclaims to be, must be who the preacher is. Phillip Brooks has it right when he said "preaching is truth through personality." The Chinese symbol for integrity is *Te*. While this could also mean virtue and goodness, the best interpretation for this is character comes straight from the heart. (Walter Earl Fluker, *Ethical Leadership-The Quest for Character, Civility, and Community*, Fortress Press, Minneapolis, p. 66). Thus, integrity is that which comes straight from the heart. The preacher's integrity is important because it informs actions and behaviors. Whenever there is the lack of power in a preacher's life, more often than not, the problem can always be traced back to some issues around integrity. Hence, it is most important to note integrity and character must become the foundation and basis for effectiveness of preaching, and often times it is integrity that preaches before the preacher ever opens their mouth to proclaim.

Preaching With Logos

The intent Aristotle had with logos as a prerequisite for listening was making certain content is a factor in whatever is said. H. Grady Davis suggested when he said, "the preacher should learn to express themselves with as few words as possible. If words are not needed, they get in the way of clearness. They cloud the picture. Thus, they should not be used." Every word should have significance, meaning, justification, and spoken with tremendous

"The preacher should learn to express themselves with as few words as possible. If words are not needed, they get in the way of clearness. They cloud the picture. Thus, they should not be used."

power. David Buttrick says, "Preachers are like photographers, setting up a series of scenes and then urging the hearer to take pictures. If sermon is homiletically structured, the hearer will end up with a film strip and not a collage." When the proper words are used in creative preaching, it will fray away from the statement made by a master in commentary to a young inexperienced preacher. When the master was asked how well a young preacher preached, this was his response, "all I can say if the text had small pox, the sermon never caught it." When the logos is treated without much thought, planning, and precision, it will often be said, "that what the text had, the sermon never caught it." Richard Lischer, in whom I was blessed to study preaching under, recently wrote a book entitled, *The End of Words*. He declares that the preacher can often confuse "style" with "persona." You may hear a preacher say "my style, is to be myself." Lischer purports that the text should call us out of ourselves, and we then find our identity in the text. He declares that as this transformation happens, the preacher offers "truth back to Truth," and it is here that preaching happens. Here are some of my favorite quotes from Lischer's writing:

The shape of the tool defines the kind of work it will do, just as the form of a story or an argument is fundamental to how it will be preached. (p.80).

- The text will tell you when to be angry, ironic, funny, or sad. It will tell you when to reason with your hearers and when to tease them with parabolic utterance, when to teach your parishioners in the synagogue, and when to soar with them to the third heaven (p. 80).

- The shape of the tool defines the kind of work it will do, just as the form of a story or an argument is fundamental to how it will be preached. (p.80).

- The preacher adjusts in matters of diction (word choice) and figures of speech not based on his or her personality, but in deference to the nature of the text. Even the most introverted cleric, will become and must become a trumpet on Sunday Morning. (p.77).

- The point of preaching is not to go back but to meet the Lord out ahead. Training in preaching, begins with training in ministry. (p. 39).

Karl Barth believed the Word of God is the Word God spoke, speaks, and will speak. The Word of God is Gospel, that is, the good word, because it is the good news. While this does not suggest fundamentalism in any way, Barth would suggest God's Word is central as the gospel, but must be expressed through prophetic preaching. The effects of sin "zaps" life. Often, this "zapping" shows up in oppression, racism, war, and poverty to name a few. There are many ills that affect the community, but the heart and content of creative preaching should be to address these conditions with prophetic hope. James Gustafon describes hope as confidence in our future. He stated, "Hope is carried by confidence that life is more reliable than unreliable, that the future is open, that new possibilities of life exist" (James M. Gustafon, *Christ and the Moral Life*, Chicago and London: Chicago University Press, 1968, p.250)

This must be the reality every preacher must hold on to. It must be at the forefront of preparation, that people are living hopeless lives. Charles Edward Booth would suggest preaching that does not have blood on it, can vastly be called prophetic preaching. It is prophetic preaching that addresses the systems and barriers that hinders humanity from fulfillment, and it is this same preaching that shows up with what Robert Smith, Jr. calls "bomb" and "balm." (Doctrine That Dance, Robert Smith, Jr., B and H Publishing Group, 2008, p. 77).

After prophetic preaching blows up the sinful conditions of racism, classism, sexism, dehumanization, injustice, and other crippling forms of culture, the "balm" is the hope that is found in the eternal truths of Christ Jesus. The hope in Christ establishes an idea that fatalities are not final.

George Fredric Watt, a Victorian era British artist, in his painting "Hope," depicts a woman playing a harp while sitting on top of the world. However, the world she is sitting is wracked with trouble, confusion, despair, and vicious malignancy. While this woman is sitting on a world that is torn and mangled, the woman is sitting top of the world with her head bandaged, but while she is wounded she is sitting on top of the world playing a harp with one string left to play. The obvious question the one would ask is, "why is she playing a harp with one string, while sitting on top of the world." The one string left remaining on the harp gives the impression that as long as she has one string left, she can still play one more tune, one more note, and one more song. 2 Timothy 4:2-4 says, "Preach the word; be instant in season, out of season; reprove, rebuke, exhort with all longsuffering and doctrine. For the time will come when they will not endure sound doctrine; but after their own lusts shall they heap to themselves teachers, having itching ears; ⁴ And they shall turn away *their* ears from the truth, and shall be turned unto fables." This is the message clearly, regardless of the attack the comes to rock your world, you must remain determined to keep playing the string you have left. Frank Thomas in his book, They Like To Never Quit Praising God, he points us to the idea that African-America preaching is derived from anguish and suffering, in which we are not always called to give answers, sometimes we should have to give the certainty of hope and God's grace. (Frank A. Thomas, *They Like To Never Quit Praising God*, p.3). This is the hope we must herald, this is the message we must minister, this is the fate we must place our faith in. Hold on to the hope.

Preaching With Pathos (Passion)

Marvin McMickle in his writing, *Shaping The Claim*, shares a story about a man names Eugene Normandy. Eugene was a conductor of the Philadelphia symphony. On one occasion while conducting the symphony very passionately, he accidentally dislocated his shoulder. What kind of passion was that, that he dislocated his shoulder doing his passion? The fundamental question all of us should raise is "what have we dislocated to do our passion?" Have we dislocated our egos, traditions, old habits to do what God has assigned for us to do? What is Passion? Passion is like a mighty current that causes a river to flow into the ocean or the rushing wind that drives the clouds across the sky. Passion moves. Passion produces. Passion brings forth what it seeks. Passion is the soul becoming one with purpose, the heart and mind becoming transformed by the revelation of God's Word and will. Passion empowers believers to bring forth the destiny God ordained for them. Passion is ignited by revelation of God and His kingdom.

Passion and emotion often operated on the same continuum. However, in the context of preaching, passion and emotion should not be confused with emotionalism.

When we seek first the kingdom of God, and God reveals His plan and purpose for us, passion ignites us to fulfill this noble call. Preaching must embrace passion. Speaking of preaching and passion. In the African tradition of preaching there was always a romantic involvement between the pulpit and the pew. There was an exchange driven by the preacher, but often inspired by the people. The preacher would often take his text, and with a hypnotic tone of preaching, he/she would preach their way into the passion of preaching. Often while holding an ear that would make for the sound monitor, the preacher's passion would take over. John Wesley declared, "if the preacher would just catch on fire, people would show up and watch the preacher burn." Passion and emotion often operated on the same continuum. However, in the context of preaching, passion and emotion should not be confused with emotionalism. Marvin McMickle says that "emotion for its own sake, is emotionalism…. there is a difference between involving the congregational emotionally, and giving in to the temptation of emotionalism." (Shaping The Claim, McMickle, p.41.) W. Floyd Breese declares, "You may lose logic to convince a person of your point of view. But emotion is required before that person will act upon that conviction." (McMickle, p. 42) Passion/emotion. However, it begins with the preacher. Jeremiah declared it was like fire in his bones. It is not a fair expectation for others to catch on fire from your preaching, if you don't catch on fire from your preaching. The fire should be evident in the revelation, preparation, presentation, even in the invitation after you preach. Passion is a crucial component of preaching.

Passion should not only drive us to preach with a vigor and energy that is complete in the gospel, but Passion should also drive us to creatively approach politics and government in our preaching. While there are many who do not believe the two should ride on each other's back, I am of the opinion one is only doing vertical preaching without horizontal relevance if a political perspective is not at least critiqued or evaluated by the gospel of Jesus Christ. There should be a balance of preaching and the evaluation of political maneuvers. Because some ministries are so prophetic and consumed with addressing such areas as politics, community affairs, social conditions and world problems, they fail to create an atmosphere for charismatic worship. On the other hand, there are some charismatic ministries that are so consumed with operating in the anointing and allowing the Spirit to flow freely, they ignore matters like racism, sexism, crime and even homelessness. The prophetic and the charismatic should compliment one another. I call this "prophecharismatic ministry." Prophecharismatic is a word I use in the ministry at Union Baptist Church to describe the old cliché that "we cannot be so heavenly bound (charismatic) that we are no earthly good (prophetic)." Any ministry serious about developing passion for the kingdom must operate in both these vain of ministry to be successful. Another way of looking at this is our model of the cross. We have the vertical relationship (charismatic) and the horizontal relationship (prophetic).

In conclusion, ethos (ethics), logos (word), and pathos (passion), are all important when doing creative preaching, and if creative ministry is to happen, it must be molded by preaching.

The Creativity of Multi-Sensory Preaching

Because there are many generations in which we live among today, if church ministry is going to be effective, it is so important we find a way to reach all generations with the gospel of Jesus Christ. One of the most profound things I love about Jesus the Christ, is he was often found ministering to all generations, it is interesting to me the same Jesus who was found as a boy speaking to the elders in the temple, is the same Jesus found as an adult begging children to come to him. Which means Jesus had a word that was relevant for all generations. Therefore, it is incumbent for the church to have this as a mission and aim to be effective among all generations.

The purpose of preaching and ministry is established to bring people back to life. It is the proclamation of the gospel.

Preaching and teaching becomes the formative foundation for establishing faith in a person. The purpose of preaching and ministry is established to bring people back to life. It is the proclamation of the gospel, with the undergirding intent to help one live in Christ. There is no church without Christ, and there is no life without Christ. This must be the central message of preaching in a post-modern world where creativity is not an option, but almost demanded. What should our preaching seek to accomplish? Leonard Sweet in his book, *Nudge*, shares a story that in days of past, it was customary for some people to be buried above ground. It was believed some people in comas were misdiagnosed for dead. Therefore strings of bells were attached to their bodies, with the expectation that if life is still there, when movement returns there will be the sounding of bells. (Nudge, Leonard Sweet, p.6,). This is gives new rise to the old adage, "saved by the bell." But more poignantly, this should also be the result of our preaching. Preaching should encompass the ability to bring life back into dead bodies, with the certainty that those who are brought back to life will ring their bells. Creative preaching causes intellectual, emotional, and spiritual bells to ring. This becomes the impetus for multi-sensory preaching and teaching. Some wise writer once declared, "creativity is the mind having fun."

The Creativity of Ear Preaching

"Creative Ear preaching" has at its root the use and purpose of language. Language becomes the mastery of ear preaching. Ear preaching has to do with the usage of words, which Aristotle refers to as the logos. Logos is the content in which we use to make an appeal to the ear. "Faith comes by hearing, and hearing by the word of God." The rhetoric of ear preaching has been etched in modernity. While one may debate and say, "no, it is not about words, but it should be your life is that preaches the message." While this is true, for a more stern interpretation of preaching, "preaching is the proclamation of the word through our personality."

Words make all of the difference in meaning and understanding. One wise writer declared, "there is a difference between lightning, and a lightning bug." While the communication of the eternal is not as simple in thought, it is our words that brings complex issues and ideas to a more digestible place. Therefore, "creative ear preaching," has to do with the mastery of words. Because it has been stated if it is cloudy in the pulpit, it is sure to be foggy in the pew. For example, if I were to preach John 3:16, "For God so loved the world, that He gave His only begotten Son, that whosoever believe in Him, should not perish, but have everlasting life," I might creatively suggest that there are 26 words in that Scripture. The 13th word highlights the "Son." The first 12 words are in reference to God, and words 14 to 25 are words are in reference to humanity. So it is Christ at the 13th word that is bridging God and humanity together. That is the purpose of Christ, to bring God and humanity together.

There are a few criteria of preaching that can bring color to "creative ear preaching." Some of those of methods are style, exegetical research, poetry, alliteration, quotes and statistics.

Creative Preaching and Style Formulation

In his book, *Four Voices of Preaching*, Robert Stephen Reid, declares there are four personas a preacher stands in when he or she is preaching/teaching. Consider the following:

THE SAGE VOICE

The Sage approach to preaching evangelistic takes the approach of raising questions for one to explore the possibilities of Christ for themselves. The sage approach to presenting Christ through the proclamation of the word is like one giving a tour guide through a forest, and along the way the guide is explaining the kind of trees and plants that are seen in the garden. On the journey, we come to a fork in the word, and the sage will say, if we choose this route, this is what we may see. If we choose another route this is what may be found. Evangelistically, the choice is heaven or hell, and the choice is yours.

THE TEACHER VOICE

The teaching voice of evangelistic preaching is represented by the ex-cathedra, an authority of the Scriptures and theological implications of the church. This voice explains Scriptures from a well-trained perspective and often approach the Bible and the Scriptures from a systematic perspective with the Scripture as its absolute resolve. This voice is often certain of their salvation experience, and is rooted in the their faith with God.

THE ENCOURAGING VOICE

The encouraging voice of preaching is a voice most needed for evangelism. This voice enters into the story of the individual, their experience, their pain, their life situation, while offering them hope by the power of the Holy Spirit, which ultimately becomes the encouraging voice. The encouragement is that God can transform, and transformation is found the Word of God.

Preaching should be like a film strip. Where scenes are portrayed, leaving the hearer empowered and strengthened to put their own movie together.

THE TESTIFYING VOICE

This voice approaches preaching with a testimony of Scriptures and one of personal experience. The testing voice comes with experience, and is often shared by one with their own personal story. However, the emphasis of the testimony is what God is able to do. The testimony is used to point to God, and not the one giving the testimony. It is in God the transformation will happen.

Creative Preaching and Exegetical Research

Exegetical research is the extraction of what is hidden within a text. Exegetical preaching has at its core creativity. Buttress says preaching should be like a film strip. Where scenes are portrayed, leaving the hearer empowered and strengthened to put their own movie together. If preaching is like putting a film together, then solid exegesis is the script for the movie. It is not content that is conferred from the outside into the text (isogesis), but it is content that is seen by the preaching personality from within the narrative. Exegesis and logos are dependent upon one another, and gives strength to the sermon that is preached.

Creative Preaching and the Use of Poetry, Stories and Illustrations

Poetry has often a tremendous support to "creative ear preaching." Poetry should not be the majority of a serious exegetical message, but it illuminates what is there. The imagery of poetry has a way of peaking imagination. This is where modern and post-modern preaching are congruent. Because we were not present during the biblical days, it takes imagery and the power of the spoken word to create a sense of our presence there. Hence, poetry if applied properly, with it's color of language, transcends the mind to a place where we have never been. Poetry can make you smell, taste, and see things that are not even there. Poetry wakes up the imagination, and stimulates the intellect to a place where words and images are lined up in the minds eye, ready to intrigue the listening ear. Consider the imagery painted with poetry.

If you can't be a pine on top of a hill, be a bush in the deep green valley, but be the best bush. If you can't be a highway, be a trail. If you can't be the sun, be a star. It's not the size of whether you win or fail, but be the best at whatever you are- DOUGLASS MALLOCK

Life is a crust of bread, a corner to sleep in a minute to smiling, and an hour to weeping. A pint of joy to a peck of sorrow, never a laugh, but moans come double, and that is life- PAUL LAWRENCE DUNBAR.

To be or not to be is the question, whether it is nobler in the mind to suffer the slings and arrows of life's outrageous fortune, or to take arms against a sea of trouble, and by opposing end them- SHAKESPEARE

Creative Preaching with Stories and illustrations

Stories and illustrations in preaching bring real life to written biblical. Creative preaching demands in its inception, a creative preacher, with a creative mind, who has a creative perspective, with a creative approach to preaching. Stories and illustrations does in the post-modern culture, what parables did for Jesus in the Bible. It helps the hearer to see. The etymology for the word illustration means to "throw light on the subject." Illustrations then are merely flashlights in a dark room. Tom Farrell in his book, *Preaching That Pleases God*, says illustrations do four things; it helps people recall, relate, receive, and remember. (p.127) Stories and illustrations should embrace detail, but the detail should not be greater than the end meaning of the story.

From a preaching perspective, salvation, deliverance, peace, hope, and joy, should be at the center of the story. While real human-interaction stories are important, they should be told as truth, but with discretion of human failure not being more significant than salvation. The preacher or teacher who reveals their weaknesses and flaws, must treat information with integrity, but always being mindful the personal struggle should not be greater than the power of salvation.

1. **PREACHING ILLUSTRATION** - CHECK YOU FIRST

Recently, I was dealing with a subject matter in Bible study about taking responsibility of our actions. In the midst of sharing this concept during the Bible teaching, I experienced a distraction. I heard what I thought was music coming through the speakers of the p.a. system. I flagged the sound technician to handle the sound of the music coming through the speakers, but he openly informed me there was no sound coming through the speakers. I openly corrected him, "yes I hear music," He respectfully said, "no pastor, there is no music coming from the speakers." But I kept hearing music, then I happened to reach in my pocket, and I discovered while teaching, I accidently hit the music app on my I-phone, and the music that was playing, was playing on me. Get this, I blamed the sound technician, and the speakers, but all the time the music was playing on me. How many times do we blame others, when the problem is really on us. We are really the problem.

Preaching Application

There are times when we need deliverance for the music playing in our own lives. The "music" of our lives could be our own insecurities, fears, complexes, or our own drama. Many times we are blaming others, when our own issues are the problem.

2. **PREACHING ILLUSTRATION- A SYSTEM THE ENEMY CAN'T HACK**

In London, England a group of young people protested against the government with masks on their faces, and called themselves hactivists. These hactivists were protesting the governments intrusion of their privacy via social media, computer spying, and government involvement in their lives. Thousands of young protestors with masks on their faces, rejecting intrusion. The protest is good, but the problem is these young people staged their protest by hacking computer systems of the government, colleges, banks, and some even accused them of the Sony saga. This caused me to raise a question for the church; Is our salvation, joy and peace, secure enough, that the devil can't hack it?

Preaching Application

How do we handle our own hactivist, and what intrusion should we protest? The enemy is always seeking to hack our faith system, therefore, it is imperative we hold on to the password, and the password is Jesus.

3. **PREACHING ILLUSTRATION- BE CAREFUL HOW YOU TREAT TUGBOATS**

Some years ago, the Carnival cruise ship was stuck at sea for several days. After several days of being stranded at sea, 2 tug boats were dispatched to push and pull the luxury liner back to shore. The tug boat is the ugliest boat on the water, yet two were dispatched to push and pull the luxury liner back to shore. When I saw this it occurred to me, you have to be careful how you treat people, because you never know when you will need a tug boat to help you get back to shore.

Preaching Application.

All of us are here because of two tug boats, one called grace, and the other is called mercy.

Creative Preaching With Quotes and Statistics

It amazes me how much color and texture quotes and statistics add to creative preaching and teaching moments. Research and documentation should always be an aim to help substantiate the argument in which you are seeking to convey. However, no sermon should be totally comprised of quotes and statistics. Integrity is also established when quotes and statistics are mentioned, knowing the information is not an original thought, it is most helpful for quotes and statistics, or date to be mentioned. Charles Spurgeon said this, "You must endeavor to make your people forget matters relating to this world, by interweaving the whole of divine truth with passing things of every day, and this you will do by a judicious use of anecdotes and illustrations." (Tom Farrell, Preaching That Pleases God, p. 129) Illustrations also come through with quotes and statistics. Consider the validity quotes and statistics add to the idea that is being conveyed.

- **A Thought About Church Vision**- Bill Hull in his book, 7 Ways to Transform Your Church says, "Less than 5% of America's pastors ever have a vision that is uniquely their own. Another 15% are merely duplicated, what they see others perform, and 80 percent of pastors are merely maintain the status quo."
- **A Thought About Trust**- Maya Angelou stated, "When people show you who they are believe them."
- **A Thought About Education**- "Rarely, do we find men and women who willingly engage in hard solid thinking, there is almost a quest for easy answers and half-baked solutions, nothing pains some people more than having to think"- Martin Luther King, Jr.

Non-biblical quotes and information adds color and depth to your preaching. Whenever using this kind of information, it is also important to cite where you obtained the material and give credit to the author for which you are quoting.

CREATIVE EYE PREACHING

Creative evangelism today must be coupled with creative eye preaching. While the "old school" preachers often practiced creative eye preaching with their tone of preaching and the imagery of their vocabulary. Today, creative eye preaching is often practiced with technology, play productions, props, human demonstrations, and other forms of preaching for relevancy.

SCREENS

Ministering in this post-modern culture is largely driven by media and technology demands for every day operation. There are approximately 8 billion people in the world, and about 7 billion people who have access to cell phones. This technological advancement in some way has arrived in the church, and one of the ways it is present is through large screens in worship. Screens in worship if used properly can provide assistance in the reading the Scriptures, singing the songs of worship, visibly seeing the worship, and it allows for even motion video clips to be used during preaching and teaching. While some people may think screens in the sanctuary makes worship more on the level of a production, its benefits far outweigh its negatives.

PROPS

Props are another form of creative preaching. Often times when the unchurched comes to church, sometimes our modern language of the faith can be quite intimidating. For example, on one particular Sunday I was preaching on the principle of tithing. While giving a tithe-10 percent of the gross income – can be difficult to understand from the onset, I decided to demonstrate tithing by using real fruit. I placed 10 oranges on a table, and then took one orange and set it aside. The one orange represented the tithe. Hearing this is one thing, but actually seeing it is something else. Props are a major benefit to the ministry in this way.

HUMAN DEMONSTRATIONS

Human demonstration is a powerful methodology for making Scriptures come alive. Jesus often used human demonstrations to make his sermons live. The woman who gave two coins, her very best became an instant demonstration for those who were not willing to sacrifice. It was Jesus who said, "this woman has given more out of her penury, than those who gave out of their plenty." It was in this way Jesus showed those in the temple that the motive of giving is often more important than the method of giving.

In Psalms 66:10-12, there is a word that says, "God cause men to ride over our heads." While the psalm is powerful as a stand alone, it is even more powerful when you put four people in a single filed line, each seeing the back of one another. Then place a prize in front of the first person. In the natural progression of things, the person closest to the front is next in line for the prize. But there are times when God will take the last person in line and move them to the front of the line, thus, they get the prize first. God caused men to ride over our heads, or to get in the front of us while we are next in line.

CREATIVE TOUCH PREACHING

Creative touch preaching has to do with preaching which motivates us to touch lives and make the sermon become real. What is evangelism if it is not about touching lives? An example of creative touch preaching, has very little to do with preaching and then saying touch your neighbor. While congregational kinesthetics are important, creative touch preaching has to do with preaching that moves people to action.

For an example, one Sunday I was preaching about the need of the church reaching beyond the church. Immediately after the sermon, I asked several people to come up to the altar and commit to going to different places in the community to evangelize. That team left the altar that day, and touched lives in the community. Creative touch preaching leads to action, implementation and a visible representation of the Word. Creative touch preaching should show up in how the church does ministry, programs, and other outreach efforts. Creative touch preaching leaves the people with something to do.

WISDOM FOR CREATIVE PREACHING

- "A preacher is not always inclined to preach a good sermon, but is challenged to always wrestle with a good thought."- *Howard Thurman*
- "Preaching is making a deposit in the hearts and minds of men and women, but also being able to write a check off of the same account."- *Robert Reid*

"The preacher in the twenty-first century will be one part theologian and one part sociologist. One part evangelist, one part mystic- a person who genuinely encounters God."- Graham Johnston

- "The preacher should learn to express themselves with as few words as possible. If words are not needed they get in the way of clearness. They cloud the picture. Thus they should not be used." - *Grady Davis*
- "I am convinced that African-American preaching has been the dominant force for our liberation, and this tradition has been essentially evangelical in scope and nature."- *Charles E. Booth*
- "The term "hermeneutic" is most fittingly applied to the process of spiritual growth. A preacher who does not have this capability flirts with boredom and loss of attention."- *Henry Mitchell*
- "The preacher in the twenty-first century will be one part theologian and one part sociologist. One part evangelist, one part mystic-a person who genuinely encounters God."- *Graham Johnston*
- "The preacher must begin with the idea that we are preaching to a secularized mind." - *Bill Hybel*
- "The contemporary climate is therapeutic, not religious. People today hunger for not a personal salvation, but for a momentary illusion of personal well-being, health, and psychic security." – *Christopher Lasch*
- "The motto of all true servants of God must be, 'we preach Christ; and him crucified.' A sermon without Christ in it is like a loaf of bread without any flour in it. No Christ in your sermon? Then go home, and never preach again until you have something worth preaching." - *Charles Spurgeon*

CHAPTER 8

THE CREATIVITY OF RELEVANT EVANGELISM

While it is important the church understands the influence of the impact of post-modernism, we must also consider what impact has a non-traditional view of the church and society had on evangelism. What is Evangelism? While there are many different definitions and explanations about what evangelism is, it is imperative we take a close look at the word evangelism. Evangelism is transliterated into the English word Evangel (Good News). The root word of Evangel is Angel (Messenger). Hence, to evangelize means to be a messenger with Good news.

If we are going to understand the dynamics and the intricate components that make up "doing evangelism," it is important we understand the value of taking risk. Evangelism is that part of the ministry, which forces you to put your confession to a cause. Evangelism at best becomes the very reason God the Father sent Jesus the son. God sent Jesus to save us. This becomes what worship should inspire. Worship should inspire us to evangelize the people, the communities, the nations, the world around us, and when we evangelize, we should deliver to the world

Evangelism is that part of the ministry, which forces you to put your confession to a cause.

the Christ who saves. We take a risk of sharing Christ with the understanding there may be results, and there many not be results. However, we should be encouraged that through it all, God will get the glory. "One plants, another waters, but it is God that gets the increase."

For evangelism to be effective and impactful for any ministry, it is important that evangelism is rooted in the Word of God, and has as a solid theological base for interpretation and understanding. Theology without evangelism is a bad product, and evangelism without theology is a worst product. Theology is necessary because if one does not have solid theology in the foundation of evangelism, it can possibly lead one to offer salvation to the world with very shallow results. Alvin Reid, in his book, *Introduction To Evangelism*, says, "Evangelism divorced from theology leads to superficial Christianity. It produces Christians who are ten miles wide and one-half inch deep" (*Introduction to Evangelism*, Alvin Reid, p. 84). Anything goes, and nothing really matters.

Hence, it is important that creative evangelism is practiced with a solid sense of what God intended evangelism to exist for. If evangelism is to be understood properly by those who are in the church, the perception of the body of Christ will be one where the church becomes a healing station, one with a storage of bandages for the wounded. Evangelism at the core is about drawing those who are outside to Christ and not ourselves. Though Peter and John told the man sitting by the gate called beautiful "to look on us," Peter was making the reference to the power of the Holy Ghost within them as a demonstration of His power. We do not have the content to sustain those whom we win through evangelism. Therefore, we must direct people to Christ and not ourselves. So what is Evangelism? The Church Growth Movement has placed evangelism primarily into three categories: presence, proclamation, and persuasion. Let us consider how these components work in concert together.

Evangelism as Presence

Sometimes the best evangelism is not in the what we saw when we go, but it is the simple fact we went. So many people today are ostracized and feel alienated even with people all around them. Therefore, evangelism is being present, but being present as an angel with good news. This should shape even our presence in the church. Because so many times when the lost, the wounded, the forsaken show up in church, they often show up at church and get hurt. The church should never master in being judgmental about people's past, size, how they dress, and even what they smell like, because an evangelistic church is not concerned about those temporal matters, but rather we are more concerned about the soul of the person God is in love with. Therefore, evangelism is often done with you being present, and God being present in you. Perhaps this is what prompted Dr. William Turner of the Duke Divinity School to suggest "many people have latched onto the shibboleth 'saving souls' as though this is something unrelated to the condition in which people live and the obstacles they must face even after they embrace Jesus." (A Journey through the Church Covenant, William C. Turner, Jr. (p.58). This is why presence is so important, because it extends the compassion of Christ to the world. Recently, I was apart of an effort to do evangelism in Ecuador, South America. It was amazing that in the mist of such poverty and ruin, and among a people who had the very least that life could offer, did not look for our group to show up with gifts and material things to survive, they were just thankful to God somebody showed up. When you are serious with evangelism, you will never take your presence for granted, because you showing up is much like God is showing up through you in the flesh. You are not God, but you do represent God.

I am reminded of a story about a church that was located in the inner city, but the members lived in the suburbs. The people would drive their luxury vehicles to the inner-city church and then get inside and lock the doors so that the "hood" can't get inside the church. One night the church caught on fire, and the people from the hood are witnessing the church on fire. While the church is burning, a brave deacon runs in and pulls a picture of Jesus off of the wall, brings it out of the church and lays the picture in the street. Now the people of the "hood" are watching this picture in the street. From among the crowd, one of the members yells out, "why are ya'll looking at that picture in the street, while our church is on fire?" The response came back, "we were just looking and saying among ourselves how it is a shame it took the church catching on fire before ya'll would bring Jesus out in the street." The power of the story is even a picture in the street can draw the ostracized closer to Him.

Evangelism as Proclamation

It was one wise writer who declared "Preaching is not just making a deposit in the hearts of men and women, but being able to write a check from the same account." In other words, as angels carrying a message of hope, it is important we proclaim a word can be held accountable. Too much erroneous proclamation has eschewed the image of the church, because in many respects, we have made the church more about the "Thingdom" and not the "Kingdom." In the "Thingdom" we show up and proclaim of the God who wants us to have things, riches and gold. While it is true God will bless us with some physical things, true proclamation points to a God who blesses us beyond things. I have discovered in my journey, the best blessings are not the blessings you can see, but it is the stuff you can't see. Paul declared it this way in 2 Corinthians 4:18, "we look not to those things which are seen, but to those things which are unseen. For those things which are seen are temporal, and those things which are unseen are eternal."

You can't put your hand on joy, but you will know it when someone possesses it. You can lay your hand on peace, but it is so radiant, it will take over a room. So alike is serenity and salvation.

S.M. Lockridge proclaimed the awesomeness of God, when he said, "the God we serve, came from nothing, because he had nothing to come from. He stood on nothing, because he had nothing to stand on. While standing on nothing, he reached out into nothing, and caught something, and hung something on nothing, and told the something of nothing to stay right there." This cosmically blessed me, that much of what God has to offer, is much of what we can't even conceive. Therefore, if we are going to share the truth of God, let us be mindful to be more eternal than material. "Silver and gold, have I none, but such as I have, I give thee, in the name of Jesus Christ, rise and walk."

The message that we must proclaim is life. Luke Powery in his book, *Dem Dry Bones*, reveals a powerful story that would depict life in the presence of death. When in March of 2000, there was a massive flood that hit Mozambique leaving thousands of lives threatened. While people were fighting to avoid the obvious reality of death, there was a woman by the name of Ms. Pedro who wanted to survive so bad, that she climbed up a tree. Having lost relatives, including her grandmother, she held on to that tree for dear life. But here is the miracle in the story, after being in the very presence of death, this young lady hung on in a tree for three days, while pregnant with child. After three days of hanging in a tree, she gave birth to a new born baby right there in the tree. Powery declares, "Life was born, in the presence of death." (Dem Dry Bone, Luke Powery, p. 97). This is the creative message that we must proclaim, while evangelizing the world to Christ. We must proclaim that there is death all around us, and the only thing that can defeat death, is that a Savior would come and die. He did come to the world, not as a flood this time, but as a Savior. Just like Ms. Petro, he hung in a tree and faced the presence of death.

However, in the midst of death, there was also the confirmation of life. Because he died, we are able to live. This is the message we must proclaim, ".... that the wages of sin is death, but the gift of God is eternal life" (Romans 6:23).

Evangelism as Persuasion.

In his book *How to Argue and Win*, Grenville Kleiser lifts up some critical points about being able to persuade. One of the main perspectives of persuading is to know your subject matter well. There is nothing like one who shows up to do evangelism to win souls to Christ, and they are not sure of Christ themselves. Persuasion begins with you. Are you sure of your certainty of Christ? Have you forgiven you of your past? Have you accepted him as Lord, knowing he still has work to do on you? These are things we must be certain of when we seek to evangelize the world. I have discovered people are often persuaded when we are persuaded. Someone has said, "if you catch on fire, others will come and watch you burn."

I have often wondered what Paul said that made Agrippa say, "This man has almost persuaded me to become a Christian." While I know Paul stood before Agrippa and preached the gospel, I'm not certain it was that alone which almost persuaded him. I believe Paul almost persuaded Agrippa, when Agrippa saw Paul was willing to forsake his tradition and custom to live relentlessly for Christ. Remember, it was Festus who declared Paul was insane, because Paul was now preaching a theology that wasn't dictated by custom, but inspired by Christ. So when Paul stood before Agrippa, as if to say I am willing to forsake all my teaching, all of my upbringing, all of the culture that is within me, to preach for this man named Jesus, it was Agrippa who said, "I am almost persuaded." Could it be Agrippa was not fully persuaded, because though he could get with the message of Christ, he wasn't willing to be as brave to leave behind the culture Christ was calling him from? Wow, this is so much like people who need to be evangelized today. They are often times very familiar with our message, but like Agrippa, they are just not willing to give up their culture. Thus, we must learn how to master the art of persuasion, and preach in such a way people are willing to give up their culture. I will discuss some of these components of preaching later on in the upcoming chapters.

Other Definitions of Evangelism

- "A concerted effort in the power of the Holy Spirit to confront unbelievers with the truth and the claims of our Lord with the view of leading unbelievers to repentance toward God and Faith in Jesus Christ" - *Lewis Drummond*

- "One beggar telling another beggar where bread is" - *N.T. Niles*

- Giving People What You Got (Jesus), After You Realized You Needed It - *Sir Walter Mack*

- "Religion is like a pair of shoes.... find one that fits for you, but don't make me wear your shoes." - *George Carlin*

- "Jesus himself did not try to convert the two thieves on the cross; he waited until one of them turned to him." - *Dietrich Bonheoffer, Letters and Papers from Prison*

- "Radical obedience to Christ is not easy... It's not comfort, not health, not wealth, and not prosperity in this world. Radical obedience to Christ risks losing all these things. But in the end, such risk finds its reward in Christ. And He is more than enough for us." - *David Platt, Radical: Taking Back Your Faith from the American Dream*

Don't wait for a feeling or love in order to share Christ with a stranger.

- Don't wait for a feeling or love in order to share Christ with a stranger. You already love your heavenly Father, and you know that this stranger is created by Him, but separated from Him, so take those first steps in evangelism because you love God. It is not primarily out of compassion for humanity that we share our faith or pray for the lost; it is first of all, love for God." - *John Piper*

- "Introverted seekers need introverted evangelists. It's not that extroverts can't communicate the gospel, either verbally or non-verbally, in ways that introverts find appealing, it's that introverted seekers need to know and see that it's possible to lead the Christian life as them. It's imperative for them to understand that becoming a Christian is not tantamount with becoming an extrovert." - *Adam S. McHugh, Introverts in the Church: Finding Our Place in an Extroverted Culture*

- "We should be more concerned with reaching the lost than pampering the saved." - *David McGee*

- "If you alter or obscure the Biblical portrait of God in order to attract converts, you don't get converts to God, you get converts to an illusion. This is not evangelism, but deception." - *John Piper*

CHAPTER 9

EMBRACING EVANGELISM FOR CREATIVE LIFE CAPACITY

Dave Early and David Wheeler wrote one of the most exciting books I have read in quite some time on the capacity of Evangelism. One of the most dangerous moves we can make as it pertains to getting the church, which is in inside to go outside, is that we limit evangelism to four steps of salvation: curiosity-wanting to know who Jesus is, conviction-convicted by the Holy Spirit, convincing- convinced Jesus died for our sins, and conversion-converted from life of sin to a life of faith. (p. 71, Early and Wheeler). However, the capacity of evangelism is much more involved and intricate at its root. In other words we are trying to fit evangelism in a bathtub, when in fact there is enough of it to have ocean capacity. Perhaps this image came in my mind because at the time of this writing I am sitting on the beach in Turks and Caicos, and it is this very ocean I am viewing that reminds me of how expansive God is, and how God desires for evangelism to wash upon our shores. In the book, Evangelism Is, consider all the capacity that Early and Wheeler would suggest evangelism has to offer to any life or any ministry. I would like to borrow

The capacity of evangelism is much more involved and intricate at its root.

their fundamental frame work for this thought about evangelism, while also giving my personal experience and interpretation of what evangelism is for me.

1. EVANGELISM IS.... THE REAL BUSINESS OF LIFE

Creative Evangelism is to become the core of our business for ministry. While there are many other things that are important and significant, evangelism should embrace every capacity of our life. If we own a business, it should be one of the core values of the business. If we teach in schools, though you can't mention the name of Jesus there, your approach to teaching should be to save a child from a life of illiteracy. If you are merely shooting ball on a basketball court, your passion should always leave room for evangelism potential. "Don't waste your life living for yourself. Don't waste it pursuing pleasure, position or possessions. Invest your life in glorifying God by the salvation of souls." (14) Another writer put it this way, "life does not consist in what a person possesses, but in what possesses him."

2. EVANGELISM IS.... OBEDIENCE TO THE GREAT COMMISSION

The Word of God declares obedience is better than sacrifice. When we seek to do evangelism, there may be places we don't desire to go, and people we don't desire to minister to. However, if creative evangelism is to be effective, you must be obedient and reach those whom God desires to reach, and remember He never needs your permission. Matthew 28:19 declares we go make disciples in all nations. It is interesting you don't have to leave your community today to reach all nations. There are many people in your community and in your city from various parts of the world. We can't be prejudice because of race or ethnic background as to who we share Christ with. Christ is available for all nations, and it is your job to be obedient to the great commission.

3. EVANGELISM IS...STANDING UP FOR YOUR FAITH, WHEN EVERY-
ONE ELSE IS SEATED

That priest that stood strong during the height of persecution of the
Jews under Hitler is a prime example of what it means to be standing
up for your faith while everyone is seated when he said, "When they
came for the Jews, I said nothing because I was not a Jew. When they
came for the unionist, I said nothing because I was not a unionist, so
when they came for me, no one said anything, because there was no
one left." These are times in which we must stand up for our faith.
When we consider the report given by David Barnett, when he stated
that 41 million Christians have been martyred, and 26 million martyred after the 1900's, it is imperative we stand up for our faith. (Zuck,
244). Likewise, approximately 4,000 churches open their doors every
year, but 7,000 close their doors. It is time we stand up for our faith.
While it is a good thing the world is becoming more global and more
faiths beliefs are being merged into our societal fabric, it becomes the
mandate and the charge for the Christian to hold up the faith.
Evangelism is boldly letting the world know for whom you believe in,
and what you believe God for.

4. EVANGELISM IS...LOVING WHOM JESUS LOVED

Presently the church where I serve, the Union Baptist Church, in
Winston-Salem, North Carolina, is located right across the street from
a halfway house. There was an ordinance put in place in our city that
said the facility would be increasing the number of inmates that would
be housed there. A meeting was called with me by some city officials
to discuss my feelings and sentiments about more inmates moving in
across the street from our ministry, and if there was any discomfort on
behalf of our ministry. My response to this question what emphatically
no, there is no discomfort or fear. As a matter of fact I began to think

about how we were about to intensify ministry opportunities, but then I began to thank God for thinking so much of us that He planted a garden right in our front yard. Creative evangelism loves whom Jesus loved, and just because a population of people makes a mistake or a wrong turn in their life, does not mean the church is not called to love them. Not only should we love those who often don't feel loved, but we should also show them loving kindness. A mother asked her son, what do you think loving kindness is, and the son said, "mother when I ask you for a piece of bread and butter, and you give it to me, that's love. But when you put jam on it, that's kindness." Not only are we called to love, but Evangelism is also putting jam on somebody else's life by doing whatever we can to make certain the Christ and the body of Christ is about love and kindness. (Zuck, 237)

5. EVANGELISM IS…SHAKING SALT AND SHINING LIGHT

As ministers of the gospel and practitioners of evangelism, there are a plethora of conditions and situations we will be called to minister to. People are dealing with family issues, loss, depression, financial crisis, identity issues, joblessness, hopelessness, and not to mention church abuse and relationship abuse. It seems the world is bathing in hurt and pain. However, it is our business to shake salt and shine light. Salt has the ability to bring out flavor and to preserve in some way. Salt helps us to get our seasoning right, and make what it is more desirable. Early puts it this way, "The world is rotten without the salty nature of the people of God. It is tasteless without the seasoning of Christianity." (*Evangelism Is*, Dave Earley and David Wheeler, p. 46). As it pertains to light of the world, Eugene Peterson put it this way in Matthew 5:14-16, "You are here to be light, bringing out the God-colors in the world. God is not a secret to be kept. We're going public with this, as public as a city on a hill. If I make you light bearers, you don't think I'm going to hide you under a bucket, do you? I'm putting you on a light stand. Now that I have put you there on a hilltop, on a light stand- shine! Keep open house; be generous with your lives. By opening up to others, you'll prompt people to open up with God, this generous Father in heaven."

6. EVANGELISM IS...LISTENING

One of the key things about the word listen is it contains within it the word silent. Both words are comprised of the same letters but spelled out differently. Therefore, I believe evangelism is not just sharing but it is also learning to listen so you will know the perspective from which you need to share. Someone asked the question to a young lad, what is the difference between listening and hearing, and here is the wise response which came back, "listening is wanting to hear" (Zuck, 231). Jerry Pipes in his book, *Building a Successful Family*, states there are some important factors we should pay close attention to when seeking to establish relationships, particularly in the home. However, these principles also speak to the listening component of Evangelism as well. Consider these factors:

- **Make Believe Listening**- Make believe listening is when you engage people for moment they are important and they matter until their discussion has no interest to you, therefore you check out. Remember, creative evangelism is not about the business of you, but it is about the business of somebody else. Therefore, if what they are talking about is important to them, you should make certain you give undivided attention to the discussion with a head nod, and interactive question, or just merely listening by applying the experience to your own life. Just because a person may not have been evangelized before doesn't mean they can't discern when you are a fake?

- **One Up Listening**- There were two men in the woods camping, and a bear happens to come right into their very camp site. One looks at the other and said, "man, I sure do hope you can out run that bear" …. the other camper, said, "man, I don't have to out run the bear, I just have to out run you." It is so interesting our conversations are much like this…. we can't listen because we are so busy trying to out run others, leaving them behind to get devoured by the bear of their condition. Evangelism is learning to listen, and not compare your victories with other people's failures.

It should not be our aim to one up anybody, but it should be our goal to arrive to place on this journey together. Your sharing helps my knowing.

Can't you hear him? "Get to stepping Gina."

- **Impatient Listening**-Impatient Listening has to do with the listener making one feel like they have had enough, and there is no more to listen to. In the Sit-com *Martin*, whenever Martin was fed up with what Gina had to say, he would simply point his finger, and tell her to get to stepping. Can't you hear him? "Get to stepping Gina." This is how we sometimes listen, in our body language, facial expressions, and even in our tone, we can communicate to others that we are tired of them crying about their condition, and because we are tired, they need to "get to steppin." Right listening should not make you tired, but it should make you more empathetic, not to mention more thankful their story is not your story. Again, evangelism is not about you, but it is always about somebody else.

- **Google Listening**- Google listening works much like Google. You type in the question, and instantaneously, you get an answer. Earley and Wheeler points to Dr. Phil in this regard, who has helped millions of people with his perspective on various life matters, however, his approach does violate a principle for those who are seeking to be effective at evangelism. "Dr. Phil" like "Google," has all of the answers. While we know Christ is the answer for all things, when a person is in crises it might not be the answer at that moment. I know I'm getting in trouble here so let me clarify. If I have an accident riding a bicycle down the street, and I fall splitting my head open. When you come to see me, this is not the time for you to share with me the Roman Road and the plan of salvation. The answer should be to call the ambulance or anybody who can provide medical assistance. So often our answers are so inappropriate and untimely, that we are offering solutions when in fact sometimes people just want you to listen. I wonder what will be the show ratings for Dr. Phil, if he just had a show where he listened and not provide answers. I would suspect the show ratings would not be too high because people are attracted to quick fixes, when in fact, much of life is not a quick fix. Don't fall for the trap of having all the answers, just take a moment and listen.

- **Social Media Listening**

Social media listening speaks to the technology driven culture for which we exist. One of the greatest challenges I have in my ministry today is learning how to minister in the company of technology. There was a time in the African-American tradition of preaching, there was a romance between the pulpit and the pew. Now technology has come into the bedroom of this sacred romance, and the distraction can hinder the attraction. Today, young people can hear you talking, and be working their fingers all at the same time. Just because they are occupied, doesn't mean they aren't listening. It's just that the moderns feel disrespected and dismissed. Hence, when you are doing evangelism it is imperative you learn a lesson from this, and remember how it actually

Creative evangelism is a process leading to an event, and the event should be that one's life is saved and fulfilled.

makes you feel that others are busy when you are talking. Evangelism is giving people your undivided attention, and not allowing distractions to come between the sacredness of the conversation. Look people in their face, remind them they have your attention, and even turn your cell phone off just so you can accomplish this one on one listening when it comes down to ministering Christ.

7. EVANGELISM IS...A PROCESS LEADING TO AN EVENT

Creative evangelism is a process leading to an event, and the event should be that one's life is saved and fulfilled. Recently, I was ministering at a church and afterwards a gentleman came to me and began telling me much history about my life. He had acquaintance with my father, and was well aware of his ministry before my father's death. The gentleman shared with me he was 98 years old, and still driving. I am asked him what was the secret to his success and him living so long. He said these words to me, "The reason I believe I made it this long, is because I was scared." Then he listed out some things for me that he was scared of. First, "I was scared not to put God first in all that I do. Secondly, I was scared to dishonor my mother and my father. Thirdly, I was scared to get drunk. Fourthly, I was scared to run to trouble, so I ran from trouble." If we had time to unpack each of these suggestions, what we will ultimately discover is life is a process leading to an event. All the things you have been through, and all the things you have seen should ultimately end up with a tremendous testimony about how you made it over. Evangelism is sharing with others what God has done for you in your process, and now the main event is that the Lord has kept you.

8. EVANGELISM IS...VIRAL IN NATURE. IT IS BOTH CONTAGIOUS AND INFECTIOUS

One of the greatest phenomenon to happen for someone who is very tech savvy is when something they post on social media of a positive nature somehow ends up going viral. Now when things can be negative against a person, and damaging to their character, it is not viral that you want. But when something goes viral, that means it is shared by so many people, spreading on so many sites, news media outlets, that the information shared can no longer be contained.

Evangelism should encompass this in many respects. The people who possess Christ, and claimed Christ as Savior should be so adamant about sharing Christ, that Christianity should be viral. The spirit that Christians possess should be so infectious, it totally takes over an environment and atmosphere. Evangelism changing the atmosphere in your city, community, home and workplace. When you show up, things should feel different, and the infectious smile and joy you have should permeate any wall of strife, confusion, and division. Evangelism should be lived in a way others catch it and walk away with the Christ you have to offer. When was the last time you posted your peace, your love, your joy, your serenity for others to see it and then share it? If you post it, I promise you someone will share it.

9. EVANGELISM IS...INVOLVEMENT NOT ISOLATION

Evangelism is not something Christians do from the sidelines, but we must be very much a part of the game. One of the challenges for many Christians is how do we be in the world, and not of the world. Maintaining holiness does not mean we isolate ourselves from the realities of the world, but it does suggest we are examples among people and in places in need of light. It is imperative Christians who are serious about evangelism must get involved in politics, sit on boards, attend P.T.A. meetings, home association meetings, and any other venue that needs to see light. Our involvement makes a difference, because our heart is right, and our perspective at the end of the day is simply doing what is right.

10. Evangelism Is...Praying for prodigals to come back home

When you carefully look at the content of the parable of the prodigal son, there are some serious arrows pointing to not so much the life of the prodigal son, but the life of the eternal son. Follow the journey, the prodigal son goes to his father and asks if he could have his inheritance to go into the world. The father grants him his request, and he enters into the world. He finds himself amongst sinners, because the word says he lived a riotous life. Most of the time when people live riotous, they often do not do it by themselves. As a result, the prodigal son finds himself in a deplorable situation like feeding swine, and the says, "I shall rise and go back to my father."

When you carefully look at this, it is evangelism at its best. Because this story gives hint to not only the prodigal son, but also to the eternal son, who also gets permission from His father to come into the world. Like the prodigal son, the eternal son dwelt among sinners and publicans. As a result of his love for the least of these, he finds himself in a deplorable condition, not a pig's pen, but a cross on Calvary. After suffering death at Calvary, and placed in a borrowed tomb, I hear Jesus saying in the words of the prodigal son, "I shall rise and go back to my father." The fundamental difference between the prodigal and Jesus, is that when the prodigal went back, he had nothing with him, but when Jesus went back to his father, he carried with him our sins.

The word prodigal actually means to spend lavishly. Evangelism is reminding the world salvation does not cost anything, Jesus already paid the price.

A Theological and Biblical Foundation for Creative Evangelism

Adrian Mouldevann in a recent teaching setting gave a very clear and precise foundation for evangelism that is theological in its approach and interpretation.

THE OLD TESTAMENT FOUNDATION FOR EVANGELISM

- **Abraham:** And I will bless those that bless you and curse the one who curses you. And in you shall all families of the earth be blessed (Genesis 12:3).
- **David:** His name shall endure forever; His name shall be continued as long as the sun; and men shall be blessed in Him; all nations shall call Him blessed (Psalms 72:17).
- **Isaiah:** And I will set a sign among them, and I will send those who escape from them to the nations, the far away coasts that have not heard my fame, nor have seen my glory. And they will declare my glory among the nations (Isaiah 66:19).

THE NEW TESTAMENT FOUNDATION FOR EVANGELISM

- Jesus: But go and learn what this means: 'I desire mercy and not sacrifice.' For I did not come to call the righteous, but the sinners, to repentance (Matthew 9:13).
- For the Son of Man has come to save that which was lost (Matthew 18:11).
- The Spirit of the Lord is upon me, because he hath anointed me to preach the gospel to the poor; he hath sent me to heal the brokenhearted, to preach deliverance to the captives, and recovering of sight to the blind, to set at liberty them that are bruised, to proclaim the year of the Lord's favor (Luke 4:18-19).

The Theological Praxis of Evangelism

1. **The Authority of Evangelism: Jesus Himself**

   Then Jesus came to them and said, "All authority in heaven and on earth has been given to me (Matthew 28:18).

2. **The Purpose of Evangelism: Make disciples**

   Therefore go and make disciples of all nations, baptizing them in the name of the Father and of the Son and of the Holy Spirit (Matthew 28:19)

3. **The Method of Evangelism: Witnessing**

   But ye shall receive power, after that the Holy Ghost is come upon you: and you shall be witnesses unto me both in Jerusalem, and in all Judaea, and in Samaria, and unto the uttermost part of the earth (Acts 1:8).

4. **The Message of Evangelism: Christ's redemptive work & the conditions for receiving forgiveness** -And said unto them, Thus it is written, and thus it was fit for Christ to suffer, and to rise from the dead the third day: And that repentance and remission of sins should be preached in his name among all nations, beginning at Jerusalem (Luke 24:46-47).

5. **The Personnel of Evangelism: You / All saved individuals**

   But ye shall receive power, after that the Holy Ghost is come upon you: and you shall be witnesses unto me both in Jerusalem, and in all Judaea, and in Samaria, and unto the uttermost part of the earth (Acts 1:8).

If any ministry is to engage in evangelism, it is momentous these tenets are made to be the foundation, and everything else accomplished in the process should reflect what is established in the Word of God. There is an urgent need for evangelism today, and it is the charge of the church to engage and open up for ways to do evangelism creatively. Consider these alarming statistics about the state of evangelism in many churches today.

Statistics That Support The Need For Creative Evangelistic Ministry

- 80% of churches in America are just maintaining the status quo.
- At the present rate of change Islam will become the dominant religion in the world before 2050
- Eight million adults who were active church goers as teenagers will no longer be active in church by the time they reach thirty.
- 2010-2012 50% of churches in America did not add 1 member to their church
- Men constitute 55 percent of the un-churched
- 95% of all Christians have never won a soul to Christ.
- 80% of all Christians do not consistently witness for Christ.
- Less than two percent are involved in the ministry of evangelism.
- 3 Million People are leaving the christian church every year.

One particular denomination did a survey on its leadership ministries. The results are as follows:

- 63% of the leadership in the church have not led one stranger to Jesus in the last two years through the method of "Go Ye" evangelism.
- 49% of the leadership ministries spend zero time in an average week ministering outside of the church.
- 89% of the leadership ministries have zero time reserved on their list of weekly priorities for going out to evangelize.
- 99% of the leadership ministries believe every Christian, including leadership, has been commanded to preach the gospel to a lost world.

- 97% believe if the leadership had a greater conviction and involvement in evangelism, it would be an example for the church to follow.
- 96% of the leadership believes their churches would have grown faster if they would have been more involved in evangelism.

"Street Level Evangelism, Where is the Space for the Local Evangelist," by Michael Parrott, *Acts Evangelism*, Spokane, WA, 1993, pp. 9-11

CHAPTER 10

CREATIVITY AND INTER-GENERATIONAL MINISTRY

With the multi-facet ways in which we can creatively do ministry today, it is important we consider how drastic changes and upgraded performance of church affects and relates to every generation. Most of the time when there is conflict among generations in a ministry, the conflict will largely stem from the lack of understanding about the core of the generations which are experiencing tension. The world of technology and computers have really come on the scene, and have caused a digital divide in the church. One may be reading the Bible from the old leather back with pages slightly falling out of the Bible, and then another may be scrolling their cell phone all in the same worship. The one's with the Bible are thinking it's disrespectful to be texting while the preacher is trying to get us to read the Scripture, not knowing that they are scrolling books and chapters of the Bible. Meanwhile, the one's with the cell phone are asking to themselves why did that lady take the Bible off of her nightstand and bring it to church. These two extremes of complete misunderstandings are all too real in an intergenerational church today. Therefore, if we are going to creatively evangelize each generation in our church today, it is imperative we know the core of each generation, and the factors that make a difference in how we interact.

Creativity has been present in every generation, and no generation should ever think they invented creativity.

Creativity has been present in every generation, and no generation should ever think they invented creativity. The word generation comes from the Latin word "genere," which means to bring forth. Every generation is called to bring forth a formation of societal stability, purpose for its people, and even a vision for the next generation. To bring forth the aforementioned requires a commitment to creativity. However, there are many people who do not free themselves enough to be creative for the next generation, because they are stuck in their own generation. Hence, vision is necessary, and it should translate into bringing forth something that does not presently exist.

To understand the validity of creativity for every generation, it is important for us to look at the events, philosophies, beliefs, and values of each generation before we can understand their contribution to the present. Peter Menconi in his book, *Intergenerational Church*, gives one of the best critiques of culture as it pertains to each generation. Much of the information provided in this book was extracted from that writing, with an infusion of other historical data that shaped some major generational themes and events. Consider some of those factors that defined generational life, theology, social activity, music, art, and fundamental communication.

Heroics or G.I Generation- 1900-1924 Many in this generation today are having memory and mobility challenges, and are leaving us daily. The church must retain the history that resides among this generation and value it. This generation housed creativity, because of so much they didn't have in earlier years, they were forced to be creative for survival. Consider some of the traits of this generation:

- This generation was shaped by the church and the church institutions. In many instances this group founded most of the churches we attend today.
- Shaped by aftermath of slavery, World War I & II, the Great Depression and the segregation of races.
- They were born before television and sound movies, rockets and traffic lights.
- The theology that shaped their faith was "leave it alone, and the Lord will fix it, after awhile."

Builders- 1925-1943 They provide muted leadership to our culture. This generation built many of our corporations and institutions, and are presently the most philanthropic people in our culture today. While they are often slow to change, they must learn to incorporate new ideas for modern day ministry.

- This group was born during the Great Depression.
- This group honored hierarchy, structure and order.
- Loyalty and dedication became their badge
- They are the wealthiest generation in American history: Leaders in philanthropic efforts.
- Those born in this era were managers and leaders of Business': and they stayed on jobs 25, 30, 40 years. This is the group that produced children who would eventually earn college degrees.
- While they were silent and often referred to as "peacemakers" in their approach, they produced leaders of the Civil Rights Movement, leaders who would become very vocal.
- They enjoyed dancing and entertainment. The two-step and jitterbug is much of this era.
- Higher percentage of people in this group refer to themselves as Christians than any other group today, and they are great supporters of missions and evangelism.

- Change can be difficult for this group; their society was constant. Tried and true works for them, and stability is most desirable.

Boomers 1944-1962 With the end of WWII, all most soldiers wanted to do was make love, and not fight. Hence, this gave rise to the boom of babies. Camelot and "funk hits" went together. However, these epic times were marked with both tragedy and triumph. The challenge of the boomers in the church are critical for transition. They see past and future, and serve as a tremendous bridge for all generations. However, their challenge will be to confront the conflict of transition and embrace change that is to come, but not solely defined by them. This generation innately questioned authority. This form of protest gave rise to the Civil Rights Movement, Women's Liberation, the Black Panther Party, the Religious Right and other groups that addressed social issues. "Though they were the first generation raised with the omnipresent television and were instrumental in introducing computers to the world, they are more likely to read for pleasure than any other generational group in the nation. The generation that made "sex, drugs, and rock-and-roll" its theme...."

- Made to go to church as children. Many left the church and returned to it when they began to have children.
- Among current lay leaders in our churches, 58% are among this generation. (39)
- This is the first generation with 50 percent of marriages ending in divorce.
- This oppositional generation gave rise to the assassination of Kennedy, King and Malcolm, and Medgar Evers.
- Their style was classified by a hippie look. Long hair, tie die shirts, bell bottom pants, the stroll, the bop, the hand jive, and other forms of relating.
- There was an experimentation with drugs, religion, horoscope, and astrology.

- Competition is as a brand for this generation. They competed for classroom space, college entry, housing, and now they are competing for grave yard plots.
- This is the forever young generation, that is now getting face-lifts, using herbal creams, and wearing contemporary styles to stay young forever.
- In 2011 the first boomer reached 65. By 2020 31 million will be 65, and by 2025 an estimated 48 million will be in this category.

Generation X'ers or Busters 1963-1981 This generation also known as "X" because they are largely unknown and misunderstood. Born during a time when the government could not be trusted, this generation wrestles with anxiety about what happens next. A generation of experimentation, this generation masterminded the computer, CNN, MTV, and globalization. The church will benefit from this generation by receiving its forward view. This generation responds to relationships that are valued and authentic.

- This generation remembers the Vietnam War, Water Gate-Distrust In Government, Carter Administration, 1979 Tehran Hostages/Terrorism Today.
- Shaped by the AIDS epidemic, legalized abortion, video games, and television. (41)
- They witnessed Jesse Jackson running for President, and Sandra Day O'Conner appointed to the Supreme Court, the Challenger disaster, and the fall of the Berlin wall and the communist threat.
- This group is not enamored with having children, as many of them were "latch key" children. Relationships are important, but they discard them at the first sign of conflict.
- Educational Guinea Pigs/Rise of ADD.

- They were growing side by side with CNN, Computers, CD's, MTV, Roots, Jaws, Rocky, Rubik Cubes, The Cosby Show, Oprah, Break Dancing,
- They witnessed the rise of Rappers as the CNN of the Community: Sugar Hill Gang, Cool DJ Herc, Grand Master Flash, Run DMC, NWA, Tupac, Biggie, Dr. Dre.
- Only 1 in 7 today are active church goers.

Millennials- 1982-2000 This generation is also referred to as "the next generation" or the 'mosaics," and could easily be called Generation Why, Generation Digital, Generation Popularity, Generation Bling Bling, Generation dot.com. This generation is truly post-modern in its theology and expression. They spend $200 billion on pop culture annually, they are both smart and skeptical of all business transactions. To engage this generation get accustomed to technology, and be patient with them understanding the past. "They worry about everything-grades, getting into the right school, finding the right spouse, choosing the right career, finding the best jobs, staying fit, and taking care of their health, the economy, the environment, and terrorism." (*Intergenerational Church*, Peter Menconi, p.42).

- This generation has been deemed the most stressed, worried, and serious generation as they began their adult life.
- Raised primarily by both parents, they were shaped by institutions.
- Disappointed by government, political, and religious corruption, this generation began to not put much trust in institutions of the church.
- This group is spiritual, but not religious
- This generation redefines family. No longer just mother, father, and children. In this generation you have single dads, single moms, blended families, grandparents raising children, muti-ethnic children, and test tube children with in vitro fertilization.

- They want to decide what is true for them, and not the institution.
- Technology Rules-Cell Phones, I-Pads, Facebook, Twitter-bites, DVD, ATM's.
- Hermeneutic of Suspicion.
- Rise of The Illuminati.
- Different Dress Code.
- This group needs unconditional love, a safe place to establishing lasting relationships, and leaders who won't lead them down the wrong path.

Generation Z- 2001 to Present This generation is a new generation that only knows the American as a war nation. This generation has been on the cusp of historical moments, not to mention, witnessing the first African-American President of the United States of America. This generation will radically redefine race relations and how the world understands opportunity.

- This generation witnessed the United States electing the first African-American President and First Family.
- This generation has been marked a war generation, because all of their life the nation has been engaged in the Middle East War.
- This generation is well informed about technology and gadgets.
- From a pastoral observation, this generation at a younger age is smarter than the last generation, and at times may seem distant. Thus, creativity is necessary for reaching this generation.

CHAPTER 11

CREATIVE PROGRAMS FOR INNOVATIVE MINISTRY

Walter Bruggemann in his book, "*Hopeful Imaginations*," considers various and sundry ways prophets of the Old Testament namely Jeremiah, Ezekiel, and Isaiah helped the people of Israel to survive the movements and transitions God conferred upon Israel. In the book he purports, "The prophetic literature is from a period when the known world of Jerusalem was destroyed in 587 BC and with it the propos and symbols which held life together…(These prophets) are cast in the difficult role of providing voice and articulation to the faith and experience of a community in exile. Their pastoral responsibility was to help people enter into exile, be in exile, and depart out of exile…to help them relinquish the old world and receive the new." (Kester Brewin, p.49)

This becomes the challenge of embracing the idea of programs being a necessary support for creativity. If we are called as church leaders to bring people out of exile, it is important we identify with the "role" of and the "importance" of programs to provide assistance in this effort. While in this writing, I have drawn much on the work of Marva Dawn, and her profound insight on worship as

Programs would be the doorway, and worship would be the great room.

being central for pleasing God, and leading others to God. I do believe her work in some way undermines and underestimates God's presence within a community gathered via a program. Consider her position in once instance in her book, *A Royal Waste of Time*, "The problem is that many congregations try to imitate them (Willow Creek Church) by turning their Sunday morning worship services into evangelistic events-without adequately understanding the difficulty of moving people from the passivity of those events into the activity of church being, from surface into the life itself." (Dawn, p.125). While I understanding whole heartedly what Dawn is addressing from the perspective of worship being more central than evangelism, I must interject that I believe she is missing that evangelism is also a form of worship, and evangelistic programming can offer worship. If we had to place the importance of creative programs in relation to worship, it would be much in the image of a house. Programs would be the doorway, and worship would be the great room. While the doorway is by no means more grandiose, significant or even larger than the great room, the doorway is the entryway into the house. Therefore, creative programming is vital for entry into the lives of people, which ultimately leads them to a place of worship and praise. For centuries in the church, creative programs have aided the work of salvation. However, because of its close alignment in many respects to entertainment, secularism, temporary presentations, attachment to money and financial transactions, programs have taken on a bad name in the kingdom of God, and in many places are deemed not necessary. Therefore, to gain a full understanding of the place of programs, it is important we understand the priority of programs from the lens of God.

The Programmatic Worship of Pentecost

One of the most significant passages in the Bible for me is in the book of Acts, second chapter. This chapter is so significant because it brings to fruition the full revelation of God's intended plan for the church through a program. It is my position the day of Pentecost was merely a program that turned into worship. Jesus tells the disciples to go to Jerusalem and wait on the promise. Now the disciples were apt enough in spiritual things to really know what the promise was, but there was something in them that moved them to be obedient. They get to Jerusalem, and are sitting in the upper room in one accord. Being in one accord does not necessarily mean they were in worship, yet evidence would lead us to believe the disciples were not often worshippers. As a matter of fact, their brand was more about critiquing, complaining, learning, and discovering. Very few places even mention them in worship. When the woman fell on her knees and took oil to anoint Christ, Judas spoke up and said, "tell her not to waste that oil, we could sell it for money." Jesus responded by saying, "leave her alone, she has prepared my body for burial." When the Children came to Jesus to learn of Him, and touch Him, the disciples tried to stop their worship. Jesus had to say, "forbid them not, for theirs is the kingdom of heaven." If the disciples had been in worship when the father brought the demoniac to the disciples, they could have healed him. But previous chapters would show they were busy trying to see who would get seats and positions in the kingdom, which was more about them and less about God. Worship was not their top priority. So on the day of Pentecost, they were more so in place to see what would happen, rather than be in a place for something to happen to them. To see what would happen is what we do at programs. We come to see something. But seeing something, could also lead to something happening. Their anticipation to see something, led God to show them something.

Look at what happens at this upper room program. There are lights, camera, and action. While they are there in the upper room in fellowship, conversation and *koinonia*, God puts on a production. God begins to meet the disciples by appealing to all of their senses. First he appeals to their hearing in the sound from heaven, as of a rushing mighty wind. Then God appeals to sight by showing them cloven tongues of fire. Then God touches their tongue, by allowing their tongues to taste fire - the fire of the Holy Spirit burned their tongue until they spoke in their own ethnic language. If this is not a production, I don't know what it is—lights, camera, and action. However, their production ultimately led them to worship. All of these souls were on fire for God in worship. A production-a program, can lead to worship, and some would even consider a program is worship because at the end of the day, it's all about God.

Programs are an essential part of any creative ministry, and a creative church should house several programs that will meet the needs of every generation in the ministry.

Programs are an essential part of any creative ministry, and a creative church should house several programs that will meet the needs of every generation in the ministry. Programs are essential because they provide fellowship, communication, an intimacy that opens one up to the environment of worship. However, worship ushers you directly to the throne room of God. Recently, I attended a conference in Baltimore with Global United Fellowship under the leadership of Bishop Neil C. Ellis, and I witnessed a program transformed into a true worship experience. The program of the conference had lights, sound, and a format for the conference participants to be governed by. However, during the praise and worship part of the program, the elevation of God's presence began to increase in strength and power. The portion of the program was suppose to last for 25 minutes. However, when there was an invasion of God's Shekinah Glory, the program never got past the praise of worship. The preacher scheduled to preach was cancelled. Pastors and church leaders were moved to such an awe, that they could not stand to their feet. Over 5,000 people were on their knees in adoration and praise. Worship broke out and people were delivered and set free. After witnessing this like never before, I was convinced that God used the program, to get us to a place of worship.

Psalm 29:2 Ascribe to the Lord the glory due his name, worship the Lord in the splendor of holiness.

The Difference Between Program and Worship

Programs are structured with great detail and direct intention	Worship is a time of being in the presence of God, and therefore must leave room for the unpredictable
Programs becomes the sign post for worship	Worship is what happens after you read the sign
Programs can embrace missions, evangelism, choir singing, food engagement, small group Bible studies, lectures for spiritual growth	Worship has the intent of engagement with God alone. It is a sole focus on what God is saying and doing, and celebrating God for who God is.
Programs may involve contracts, rehearsals, committees, planning efforts, timing, and execution.	Worship may have a plan and may have intended timing, but God's spirit may impede and takeover.
Programs are often more entertaining and appeals to our need to see, hear, smell and touch.	Worship involves an engagement with soul and spirit, but can be entered with what we see, hear, smell, and touch
Programs is the marketing of a content	Worship is the content, and what the church should ultimately want people to do after the program
Program is often used for the purpose of branding or achieving a particular goal and purpose	Worship is difficult to brand because it is difficult to know when it will happen and how it will happen. Once it happens, it may never happen that way again.

Programs may not be deemed successful if people do not have maximized purpose	Worship is not about success. Worship is about an experience. Only God determines the success

The fundamental intent of presenting the two extreme differences between programs and worship is to explain the differences, while also showing where the two may be complementary. In short, if we are going to be serious about creative model ministry, we must know a program is often needed to serve as a platform for worship to happen. If we were to compare programs and worship to the design of a home, the program would be the front porch, and worship will be the great room. The program becomes the entry way, for God to bless you in His house in His own way.

CHAPTER 12

EFFECTIVE PROGRAMS FOR ESTABLISHING A CREATIVE MINISTRY

THE PURPOSE OF JAZZ NETWORKING MINISTRY

The fundamental purpose of the Mid-day Jazz Network is to evangelize the city by providing an opportunity for business professionals and local community leaders to come together at the church for inspiration and motivation to impact the work place.

PRACTICAL STEPS FOR MINISTRY IMPLEMENTATION

1. Organize a group of individuals in your church who work in various locations throughout the city.
2. Have the committee to invite people from their work locations and get the word circulated about this ministry.
3. The program should last for 1 hour, or the duration of a sufficient lunch schedule. The program format should be as such:

Opening and Welcome- 5 Minutes

Motivational Message- 15 Minutes

Featured Business and Entrepreneur- 5 Minutes

Workplace Updates and Announcements-5 Minutes

Lunch and Jazz Fellowship/Networking- 30 Minutes

A light lunch should be shared, and the Jazz music can be live or recording. The Jazz component is important because it invites a different atmosphere for the occasion. Gospel Jazz is plus for a function like this.

EXPECTED OUTCOME

To have people become more affiliated with your ministry, and inspire the participants to become motivators and spiritual change agents in the workplace. This will also be an opportunity for the Kingdom of God to network by sharing resumes, business cards, and other information for professional success

EXPECTED CHALLENGE

To market this ministry within the church in a precise way, so the members who participate meet the targeted requirements. Be careful about telling people not to attend if they are not professionals, so maybe extending the idea to people who just need inspiration in the workplace will be a good thing to do. Simply use this moment to inspire.

FIRST FRIDAY FOR THE MILLENNIALS

The fundamental purpose of a First Friday is to have a summer series of alternative worship services throughout the summer. This ministry is intended to provide an alternative choice of entertainment for young adults who do not desire to be in the night club or the scene of hanging out.

PRACTICAL STEPS FOR MINISTRY IMPLEMENTATION

1. Organize a group of young adults and some seniors to plan three events during the first Friday of the summer months.

2. Incorporate seniors and youth in the activities and provide a ministry that appeals to all ages while targeting young adults.

3. Invite local choirs, groups, dancers, steppers, and gifted vessels from other churches in the city to foster fellowship and contact evangelism for others.

4. Advertise on the local secular radio station, the intent is to reach the unchurched.

5. Have the programs organized and executed with proficiency. The program should last approximately 2 hours.

EXPECTED OUTCOME

To have people to enjoy creative forms of ministry like gospel groups, Christian Jazz Artist, Poetry Reading, Spoken Word, Play Productions, Outdoor Cookouts, and even a Christian Dance Gala.

EXPECTED CHALLENGES

Motivate members who do not accept the alternative forms of ministry to understand the need of reaching young adults through this method. Involving seniors in the planning can be helpful.

ARTIST DRAWING DURING WORSHIP

The fundamental purpose of this ministry is to express the glory of God during Art presentation in the presence of worship. We often celebrate the ministry of preaching, singing, dancing, and miming during worship, but very seldom do we understand drawing and creating portraits as a gift to be shared during worship.

PRACTICAL STEPS FOR MINISTRY IMPLEMENTATION

1. Contact a local artist preferably someone who is mature in the faith.

2. Set the artist up in a location where they can be seen drawing during worship.

3. Ask them to interpret what the spirit is leading them to draw, at the end of worship, allow them to explain what the spirit shared with them, while showing the congregation their drawing.

EXPECTED OUTCOME

To have people to better appreciate Christians who have the gift of drawing. Also, there will be a better appreciation of the interpretation of worship through this art forum.

EXPECTED CHALLENGES

Motivate members who do not accept the alternative forms of ministry, and it is possible that the artist can be distractive if he/she is not located in the right place.

YOUTH TAP DANCE MINISTRY

The fundamental purpose of worship in this formation is to express the glory of God during a moment when youth Tap Dance in worship. Many churches are using liturgical dance and miming in their worship services, but a different creative twist for young people will involve tap dancing for His glory.

PRACTICAL STEPS FOR MINISTRY IMPLEMENTATION

1. Contact a dance instructor preferably a person who is mature in the faith.

2. Identify youth who have an interest

3. Allow youth to tap dance while gospel music is playing during their performance

4. Rent wood panel flooring if you have carpet in the sanctuary, and place the panel flooring where the performance will take place.

EXPECTED OUTCOME

To have youth connect to worship differently, and give youth more opportunities for involvement.

EXPECTED CHALLENGES

The placement of the wood flooring could be a challenge, but even if you do not have wood flooring panels, let it happen anyway. It's all about getting people creatively engaged.

GOSPEL ICE CREAM TRUCK MINISTRY

The fundamental purpose of an Ice Cream Truck Ministry is to evangelize the city by providing ice cream throughout the community, while making contact with residents when passing out tracks and information about the church and ministry.

PRACTICAL STEPS FOR MINISTRY IMPLEMENTATION

1. Set aside an opportunity for your ministry to provide resources to purchase a van and upgrade the van to be an ice cream truck with a fun wrapping or paint job. The estimated cost is about $30,000.00

2. Involve the youth of your church to name the ice cream like: comfort chocolate, victory vanilla, sanctified strawberry, praise pops, and other fun names.

3. Get volunteers from the church to drive the van throughout the week, and also allow the van to be present on Sundays and during other special events throughout the city.

4. Secure a license from the city or county to drive the van and offer ice cream at restricted areas throughout the city.

5. Contract with an ice cream vending company to reload your stock, and have a very good inventory system in place.

EXPECTED OUTCOME

To have people become more affiliated with your ministry, and to spread the gospel of Jesus Christ while using ice cream as an "attention getter" for a greater salvific purpose.

EXPECTED CHALLENGES

To get enough revenue from the ministry to support van maintenance and gas as well as find the areas of your city that are a "hot spot" for the provision of ice cream.

CORNER 2 CORNER DRUG DEALERS AND STREET LIFE CONFERENCE

The Fundamental Purpose of a Corner 2 Corner Drug Dealers and Street Life Conference is to have men and women who live a life of destruction to themselves and others to gather in the church for inspiration, motivation, correction, and life strategies that will aide them in being the people that God called them to be

PRACTICAL STEPS FOR MINISTRY IMPLEMENTATION

1. Organize a group of individuals in your church who sense a call and a passion to reach those who are living the street life. Former drug dealers and people living the street life will be ideal.

2. Organize this group to gather strategies and ideas for shaping the conference and discussing the pros and cons of such an effort.

3. Call a meeting with politicians, judges, supporting agencies, pastors and other church leaders to get their input and investment into having a ministry like such in the city. Do not expect support from all, but seek to inform and even partner with those who are willing

4. Contact the Union Baptist Church, Winston-Salem, NC, for a personal training session for you church and community 336-724-9305 x.222. This session will present for you the program format, the letters to be written, cost factors for the conference, pros and cons of participants, and the method of follow up after the conference.

EXPECTED OUTCOME

The expected Outcome from this ministry is to have men and women to see their life and community in a greater way. You can expect your ministry gaining the reputation of being a "real" community church, and that your church is living what they are preaching. Expect some members already in the church to be excited about such a ministry, likewise, look for those who may fear this population being the closely connected to the church.

EXPECTED CHALLENGE

To gather a committee of people inside and outside of the church who will stand with you while you seek to implement such an innovative ministry. Also, getting participants to trust your intentions are pure.

SWEAT SUIT SUNDAYS

The Fundamental Purpose of a Sweat Suit Sunday is to emphasize in a visible way the importance of physical exercise for the congregation. This worship service is still centered around the traditional form of worship, however, on this Sunday the members are encouraged to wear sweat suits, and a leader trained in health and physical education will give health tips about diet, medical examinations, blood pressure, diabetes, and top it off, 5 minutes of exercise is done right in the sanctuary.

Practical Steps for Ministry Implementation

1. Teach and Preach sermons on the importance of physical health for at least two months.
2. Organize a health fair to engage the congregation into the physical health status.
3. Identify a person who has the professional expertise and spiritual wisdom to lead the congregation into exercise for all ages of the congregation.
4. Establish which Sunday your church will have exercise in the sanctuary and ask all members to wear sweat suits on that Sunday.
5. Do testimonial appeals of people who are actually progressing physically because of their new-found interest in exercise.

Expected Outcome

To have the congregation to understand that the physical care of the body is just as important as the spiritual care of the body. The sweat suit visibility is a monthly reminder that movement of the physical body is vital to living. Add components to this ministry by starting weekly Zumba classes, group walking on the track, and reserve a room for stretching and meditation throughout the week.

Expected Challenge

To get some members of the congregation to understand the sanctuary can be used for a place to exercise for five minutes once a month. Finding qualified people to lead the group exercise with spiritual insight can be a challenge.

SPANISH SPEAKING SUNDAY

The Fundamental Purpose of a Spanish Speaking Sunday is to move the church to an awareness of cultural differences and sensitivities. With the growing population of the Hispanic community, this worship service is designed to confirm community and move the church to being open to different cultures by learning language of the Hispanic community.

PRACTICAL STEPS FOR MINISTRY IMPLEMENTATION

1. Teach and preach messages before the congregation on the importance of expanding the definition and reference of community.

2. Identify people in the congregation who speak Spanish fluently, and make them a part of your planning team. If there are not people in your congregation who speak Spanish, contact a local college or high school for partnership in this effort.

3. Plan 10 minutes in your worship for this exercise, and you may change the exercises from month to month. Teach phrases like;
   a. Buenos dias - Good Morning.
   b. Hola, me llamo - Hello, my name is.
   c. Como se llama usted? - What is Your Name?
   d. Estoy Bein - I am Fine.

4. For those who desire a more critical understanding of the Spanish language, the church may consider offering classes throughout the week for those who need to learn Spanish for their job, travel, or educational opportunities.

EXPECTED OUTCOME

To have the membership to learn Spanish words and phrases during the worship service that will enhance their communication with the Hispanic community. It is desired this ministry will make people feel comfortable is sharing, while also creating an atmosphere that will be inviting to other cultures, namely the Hispanic community, which is the lead to other possibilities.

EXPECTED CHALLENGES

The challenges of doing out of the box ministry like this is some members understanding the relevance of such programming. Expect some members not to participate, or even mumble about having this done during worship. But understand this may be a sentiment of the attitude towards the culture of the people and not the program of the ministry. Finding people who speak Spanish could be a challenge, but refer to the support of other agencies who can assist in this regard.

MASS WEDDING CEREMONY

The Fundamental Purpose of a Mass Wedding Ceremony is to use a wedding ceremony as an innovative evangelistic outreach method. This service is designed to give couples who are living together or in a dating situation an opportunity to have a full wedding at the expense of the church.

PRACTICAL STEPS FOR MINISTRY IMPLEMENTATION

1. Place an announcement in the church bulletin and community newspaper about the plan of a mass wedding ceremony. This announcement should be done 6 months in advance.

2. Require the couples go through at least 4 mass counseling sessions. i.e., explaining salvation, the role of the church, God's intention of marriage, finances, intimacy, communication, family dynamics, etc.

3. Have couples wear formal or semi-formal attire. Preferably the women in white or light colors and the men in dark suits with bow ties or neck ties.

4. Plan one or two rehearsals. Have the wedding committee of the church or volunteers assist in planning and executing of the wedding.

5. Be creative about planning the worship, and have all couples to recite vows at the same time, pronounce at the same time, kiss at the same time, and announce each couple individually.

6. Plan a mass wedding reception, and assign a couple from the ministry to walk with the couple and help disciple them for at least a year.

7. *Open the ceremony to those who desire to rededicate their marriages.*

EXPECTED OUTCOME

To have couples to make a wrong relationship right by openly confessing vows of love and commitment to one another. Once couples are moved away from the guilt of their sin, there is a more compassionate view of the church, and a willingness to be a part of the church.

EXPECTED CHALLENGE

To have couples to enter into pre-marital counseling that may not have a Christian foundation or even an understanding of what it means to be married as a Christian,

HONORING PASTORS, POLITICIANS AND COMMUNITY LEADERS

The fundamental purpose of honoring Pastors and Politicians in a special program is to recognize the work and labor of these two constituents while celebrating the longevity of relationships that exists with these two entities.

Practical Steps for Ministry Implementation

1. Organize a group of individuals in your church that will be objective in choosing people to be honored for that particular year.

2. Choose five pastors to be honored and five other community leaders to be honored.

3. Organize a special worship service with the individuals being honored present. Have the biographical summaries and celebrated highlights printed for the sake of time. Appoint a person to read the highlights or use the video screen to aide this effort.

4. Present the honorees with a plaque, and give them 2 to 3 minutes for comments.

Expected Outcome

To celebrate pastors and community leaders who have served well and consistently to be honored every year in your ministry, To strengthen relationships in the church and the community, while recognizing the work of these individuals during a worship service, and giving a plaque in their honor.

Expected Challenge

To have a committee that can celebrate other ministries and other leaders. Also a challenge may be to organize the format for selection, and ways to address those who were not honored in that year.

Social Media for Creative Application

The Purpose

It is important as you seek to do ministry outside of the box, you keep up with the technological advancement of the culture, and the ways in which the world is experiencing change. Social Media is one of the ways in which the world is highlighting experiences and demonstrating realities that are often valuable lessons to learn from. Social Media is an awesome way to tap into the visual sense for learning life and biblical application. Social Media can be a creative and wonderful tool for conveying a message to the church and the world today.

1. Identify the overall message you want to convey in your listeners and viewers.

2. Decide what is the best social media outlet for your ministry and began to research it. Learn the pros and cons of its operation.

3. Gather congregants who may have an interest in social media to discuss effective ways to manage this ministry for the church.

4. If you are a leader responsible for preaching and teaching, use videos, music, screens, and other visuals for effective technology ministry.

THE EXPECTED OUTCOME

Using technology will indeed get a different response than the traditional forms of communication. For the elderly generation it might be quite different for them to see YouTube being used in a sermon or teaching lesson. On the other hand, the younger generation will love your use of social media for ministry purpose

THE EXPECTED CHALLENGES

The challenge with using social media for ministry is that social media changes so often. Therefore, to be relevant and effective, it is important you identify someone who can manage this ministry and keep the church relevant in this regard.

CHRISTIAN DANCE PARTY

A Christian Dance Party can be one of the most controversial programs you provide for your ministry. However, there is a way to do this kind of ministry with decency and order. This kind of ministry is strictly about fun and fellowship. It is a ministry to allow primarily people of all age to dance in a Christian environment among Christians. There are many fun songs that motivate people to move their bodies that are not church songs, like the electric slide, the cha-cha, and the wobble. While this is not traditional church music, it does have a way of presenting a different side of the church, a church, which is sociable and still saved.

STEPS TO IMPLEMENT THIS MINISTRY

1. Do Bible studies and preach sermons and the seeing God beyond the norm.

2. Secure a nice hotel for the dance party that will represent good taste and class.

3. Invite a DJ who is saved, and has wisdom about the taste of selection of the proper songs to play at this party.

4. Dress up the occasion by requesting this to be a "black tie/formal affair" or standard church attire. Have monitors as hostess to look for any clothing too revealing and have training sessions on how to approach such situations. We invited a referee to blow the whistle on dancing that was too illicit.

5. Have the DJ to play several group dancing songs that will allow collective fun, and soul train lines to form.

6. There will be no alcohol, champagne, or wine offered at the Christian Dance Party. This provision can quickly shift the focus from "fun" and "fellowship" to irreversible public relations for your ministry.

7. At the end of the dance have everyone gather in a circle, and have the pastor to remind the attendees this one-time event does not give people a license to "party" every weekend, but this is a gathering among the "Saints" with the sole purpose of fun and fellowship. Close with prayer and be dismissed.

The Expected Outcome

The expected outcome of this ministry is "fun" and "relationships." This kind of gathering will draw people of all adult ages, and though people are having fun dancing among Christians, they will be looking for ways to still remain "holy." Expect to find people you thought stayed on their knees in prayer exercising to the max their privilege of free will and truly having fun.

The Expected Challenge

The challenge for a ministry like this is theological. Finding a way to justify this kind of activity from the Scriptures, while convincing people who are "naysayers," it is simply about "fun" and "relationships." This is not too theological, but it is practical. Let people find the joy in salvation in all things.

Interdenominational Unity Prayer Gathering

The fundamental purpose of the City-Wide Unity Prayer Gathering is to create an environment of worship, unity, fellowship, prayer and community cooperation among the churches and pastors in our city/county. This prayer gathering is designed to be inter-denominational and inter-racial, and would seek to embrace all churches regardless of their secondary Christian doctrinal beliefs, theological positions and interpretations of the Scriptures.

This prayer gathering is intended to announce to the larger community of Winston-Salem our churches stand as one body in Christ Jesus.

STEPS FOR IMPLEMENTATION

- Gather a core team of community pastors and leaders who represent almost every denomination in your community. Example: Baptist, Methodist, Pentecostal, Apostolic, Episcopalian, Catholic, Church of God in Christ, Non-Denomination, etc. This will be the lead team, and representative will serve as recruiters for their denominations. With the core team establish these terms and doctrinal beliefs for all who participate:

PRIMARY BELIEF

I believe in God the Almighty, Creator of the heaven and earth. I believe in Jesus Christ, His only son, our Lord. He was conceived by the power of the Holy Spirit, born of the virgin Mary, suffered under Pontius Pilate, was crucified, died and was buried. He descended to the dead, and on the third day He arose again. He is seated at the right hand of the Father, and He is coming again to judge the quick and the dead. I believe in the Holy Spirit, the church universal, the communion of saints, forgiveness of our sins, the resurrection of the body, and life everlasting. Amen.

SECONDARY BELIEFS

Right Wing/Left Wing Politics
Positions of the Republican Party
Positions of the Democratic Party
Abortion
Stem Cell Research
War In Iraq
Women in Ministry

Men in Ministry

Historical Racial Factors

Sectarian Prayer- vs.- Non-Sectarian Prayer

Establish The Intent Of The Day

To lead the people of God into a spirit of unity, and celebrate the areas of common interest rather than differences.

- To offer a spirit of optimism, and lead the people into an understanding of cooperation and inter-relatedness.
- To help people to understand secondary issues are important, but the primary issue is what gives us unity.
- To pray for the citizens and its affairs.
- Secure date, time, and a neutral location for all who participate; a convention center, hotel, or an event center, which will allow all denominations to feel welcomed and included.
- Have a community church interest meeting, and have the core group to invite as many churches in their denomination to attend the interest meeting.
- Establish a unity choir, select musicians of the participating church to organize the choir, and even consider including dance ministries, and stringed instruments.

Organize the Program Format

10:30am The Unity Symphony for God

10:40am The Procession of the Choir and Musicians

10:55am The Procession of Ministers

11:00am Call To Worship

Invocation

Choir and Congregational Hymn- "Holy, Holy, Holy"

Old Testament
Old Testament Hispanic Interpreter

New Testament
New Testament Hispanic Interpreter- Victoria Hanshel

Pastoral Epistles
Pastoral Epistle Hispanic Interpreter

Welcome
The Mayor
The Occasion

(The Appeals and Prayers will Be 2 Minutes Each)
Prayer Appeal for Elected Officials
Prayer for Unified Vision and Cooperation
Prayer for Staff and Personnel in all Departments of City/County Gov.
Prayer for Equality and Justice in Judicial System

Prayer Appeal for Community
Prayer for the Citizens of the City/County
Prayer for Safe Neighborhoods and The Deterrence of Violence and Crime-
Prayer for Community Development, Businesses, Medical Facilities, Schools, Colleges and Universities

Community Choir and Dance Ministry Presentation

Prayer Appeal for Citizens and Human Relations

Prayer for Neighborhood Diversity and Cultural Embracement-
Prayer for the Destruction of Racism, Sexism, Classism, and Prejudice
Prayer for Homeless, Incarcerated, the Poor and Neglected

Prayer Appeal for the Body of Christ

Prayer for Unity Among the People of the Churches
Prayer for the Unified Body of Christ
Prayer for All Clergy and Church Leadership

Introduction of Special Guest- Dean Leonard
Community Charge- National Notable Speaker that can speak to all
denominations and all communities (Example- Dr. Gardner C. Taylor)

Choir And Dance Presentation and Lighting of the Unity Candle
The Benediction

GROUND RULES FOR PROGRAM PARTICIPANTS

> Every program participant must be in the holding area at 10:15 a.m. with robe/vestments for the occasion.

> If you are not clergy but serve on the program, please where black and white for the day.

> Every presenter/speaker will have a maximum mic time of two minutes. Please use your mic time wisely rather than participating in loose conversation.

> If you go over two minutes, the worship leaders will tap you on the shoulder indicating your time is up. Please practice discipline and obedience.

> Because of the various traditions, denominations, and interpretations that will be gathered on that day, please be mindful and

respectful of other theological positions, and craft your words in a fashion suitable for such a gathering. No disrespect to any denomination will be tolerated at any time. However, be free to be yourself, and pray in your tradition.

> Everyone is asked to please follow the program and be ready to present at your designated time.

> Those who are rendering prayers, please be mindful to pray for your category, and your category only. The categories have already been carefully selected and prayed over.

THE EXPECTED OUTCOME

A gathering like this will develop enthusiasm throughout the community. The outcome of such a gathering will certainly enhance relationships, tear down racial barriers, encourage churches to look beyond stereo-types, and increase the interaction between pastors, politicians, and community leaders.

THE EXPECTED CHALLENGE

Do not look for every pastor and church to get on-board initially. Many churches are comfortable with their primary relationships and may not take interest in developing others. However, do not allow the lack of their participation to hinder the process. Finances can be a challenge. However, a plan will be discussed later to introduce a plan for accomplishing the budget. Communicating the plan with language, which is amenable for every denomination could be a challenge, but can certainly be worked out through conversation, meetings, and dialogue.

COMMUNITY CANCER SURVIVORS PARADE

There is no greater reward than giving people strength and encouragement in the time of an illness. What better way to encourage people who are living with cancer or caregivers of those who are living with cancer than to have a collective body of people march the streets by faith believing God to be a healer of all cancers and diseases.

1. Organize a group of cancer survivors and caregivers to help execute the plans for the march.

2. Identity a route approximately 1-2 miles, and file a license to march while securing the involvement of the local public safety. Announce the march is for survivors, caregivers, and in memory of those who have battles any type of cancer. The following colors are the representation for various forms of cancer:

Grey: Brain Cancer

Green: Kidney Cancer

Dark Blue: Colon Cancer

Yellow: Liver Cancer

Purple: Pancreatic Cancer

Black: Melanoma (Skin cancer)

Orange: Leukemia

Periwinkle: Stomach Cancer

Lime Green: Lymphoma

White: Lung Cancer

Lavender: General cancer awareness

Encourage those who can't walk to drive cars, ride bicycles, or other forms of transportation for representation. Invite bands, cheerleaders, dance groups, auxiliaries from the church, business organizations, to participate and bring excitement to the crowd.

THE EXPECTED OUTCOME

When a march like such is announced and made available for the entire city, expect people of all ages to participate. Most cancers are represented by a color, for example, Pink is the color for Breast Cancer, Light Blue for Prostate Cancer, Teal for Ovarian/Uterine Cancer, Gold for Childhood Cancers, etc. Imagine all of these colors represented with signs and pictures of loved ones who are surviving, and those who are already resting with the Lord due to this illness.

You expect miracle testimonies because of the prayers of the people who march the streets by faith.

THE EXPECTED CHALLENGE

To have plans well executed for the march, and considering all details for safety precautions.

YOUTH CHARACTER FOOTBALL LEAGUE

THE PURPOSE OF CHARACTER DEVELOPMENT PROGRAM OF THE CFL

The fundamental purpose of the CFL (Character Football League) is to provide youth a positive educational, character, and athletic experience, while addressing the issue of childhood obesity, gang violence prevention, personality, esteem development, and healthy social enhancement skills. This program is also designed to provide youth with an opportunity to play sports in a Christian environment, which becomes another forum to united families, evangelize souls, and market the ministry in the community.

PRACTICAL STEPS FOR MINISTRY IMPLEMENTATION

1. Organize the CFL Score Board for the purpose of facilitating the vision of the CFL ministry, and address the critical and detailed matters. The Score Board should serve as a functioning commit-

tee that will further organize, develop, critique, and analyze the operation of the organization.

2. Identify a CFL commissioner who will maintain the responsibility of ensuring the CFL will operate in an efficient manner, and will be charged to always be mindful of issues regarding <u>legality, ministry protocol, budgeting matters, coaches training, field set-up, and player safety procedures. pre-post plans</u>. The commissioner will be working close with the CFL Board to make certain that ministry operation is consistent with regular programming efforts of the ministry.

3. Identify coaches within the church and outside of the church. Establish an interview process, and establish the protocol for training.

4. Find a football field that will serve as the home field. Consider a school field that will share their resources with you upon availability, or consider another facility for practice and game days.

5. Decide how many teams will be a part of your league, how many youth will be needed for each team, discuss the cost for each player. Our cost at Union Baptist Church is $125.00. Advertise and recruit for youth to sign up for the league, and thoroughly discuss vital details such as practice and game schedule, role and responsibilities for practice and game days, cost of uniforms, helmets, and colors for each team. Rules and regulations are a must.

6. Have youth to attend "huddle sessions" which are classes designed to shape character by discussing educational goals, peer pressure, gang pressure, sex, the problems with drugs and alcohol use. These classes can be done in 3 hours, and facilitated by people with information in these areas. Every youth must attend before putting on a football uniform.

7. Solicit community support for resources that will help aide the cost for: scholarships for youth who cannot afford the cost, sound system, golf carts to transport equipment/injured players, scoreboard, cost for referees, etc.

Contact the Union Baptist Church, Winston-Salem, North Carolina for workshops and more detailed information on how to organize the Character Football League.

THE EXPECTED OUTCOME

As a result of this ministry you can expect to see the confidence and the personality of the youth to flourish. The athletic skills of the youth will be developed, and young people will be nurtured to wholeness that will steer them away from drugs, alcohol, gang activity, and other forms of destruction. In homes where parents are not living in the same household, this is the one forum where both parents will be present to give support to their child who is participating in the CFL.

EXPECTED CHALLENGES

Getting the church to commit to the start up cost for the league. Finding committed volunteers, recruiting youth who will find interest in your program, especially if there is an existing league in your community.

COMMUNITY BASKETBALL, SOFTBALL OR FLAG FOOTBALL FUN-RAISER

PURPOSE

Sports and recreation is a tremendous way of bringing people together is a fun competitive manner. This game is designed to give the body of Christ a relief, while watching pastors and church leaders from various churches come together and exemplify a visible picture of unity and community.

STEPS TO IMPLEMENT THIS MINISTRY

1. Organize a meeting with Pastors and church leaders to explain the concept of the FUN-raiser

2. Get the teams organized, and ask participants to check with their medical doctors before playing these sports if this is not a part of their regular routine.

3. Market this event on the radio, television, and newspaper highlighting for the community to come out and witness pastors and church leaders playing sports.

4. Ask coaches from a college or high school to serve as the coach of these teams which will bring another level of excitement. If there is a professional sports figure from your community, invite to serve as honorary coach or coach of the team.

5. Get referees to volunteer for the game, and to add some excitement to the day invite a local college or high school band to perform.

EXPECTED OUTCOME

Get a large enough facility because the response to this game between pastor and church leaders will draw a major crowd from various places in the community. If you use the forum to raise money for the homeless, scholarships, youth program, etc., the cost should be reasonable and expect to reach your goal.

EXPECTED CHALLENGE

The challenge is to make certain everyone involved participates, and the purpose is clearly explained this is not a game of hostile competition, but rather is a game for fun and community solidarity. Another challenge could be what benefit should be supported from the proceeds.

CHURCH SHOE-SHINE BOOTH

A Shoeshine Booth in a church may be unheard of, but it makes all of the sense for world for the Kingdom of God to consider this innovative idea. Many men and women still dress in Sunday's best to attend worship and do not have the time to get their shoes shined. This ministry is about convenience, and ministering to people while they are getting their shoes shined.

STEPS TO IMPLEMENT THIS MINISTRY

1. Have a shoe shine booth purchased or built and located in a high traffic area in the church.
2. Identify people who have an interest in shining shoes and train them to shine.
3. Advertise every Sunday for individuals to support the ministry, and give a generous donation for the service provided.
4. Hire people who get delivered from your "Corner- 2 -Corner Conference." When people give up a life crime, drug dealing, prostitution, and jail residency, this will be a good start back to restoration.

THE EXPECTED OUTCOME

A great name for this ministry would be "Soul to Sole" because with this ministry you can expect for people to have their souls ministered to while their shoe sole is being cleaned. You can expect for the shoe-shine booth to become a hub for men and women to hang-out, as well as an opportunity to create jobs for members in your church. In our ministry whatever donation the individual who is shining receives, they keep. What a great opportunity in difficult times.

THE EXPECTED CHALLENGE

The challenge is to keep those who are volunteering busy and those who need shoes shined coming. Buying a booth can be expensive. However, if you can get someone to build a booth this cost could be reduced significantly.

SKATE RING WORSHIP

The fundamental purpose of Skate Sunday is to give young people an alternative experience of hearing and receiving the word in an environment that is fun and relevant for them. This worship serve is held quarterly at Union Baptist Church, and comprises of praise and worship, preaching, teaching, and skating to gospel music.

1. Call and request use for the skating ring on a Sunday morning. Most facilities are not being used at that time.

2. Identify a team of people to plan and organize this worship experience at the skating rink

3. Have youth to invite their friends which becomes a form of outreach and evangelism. Advertise and inform parents to drop the children off and then they themselves come to adult worship at the church. Adults parents should not be at the skating rink.

4. Get the health ministry involved by asking an attendant to be present at the skating ring in the event of an accident.

5. Establish a set up team and a break down team to handle the care of the equipment used for the worship moment.

EXPECTED OUTCOME

Expect for more youth to show up on this Sunday, and expect for the youth to have an interest in ministry and church life beyond the event.

Expected Challenges

- Having enough youth workers to cover the facility.
- To get parents comfortable enough to leave their children in that environment with youth workers.
- Having enough skates to accompany the youth.

Community Baby Dedication

The fundamental purpose of the city-wide baby dedication is to give babies who have never been touched, prayed over, or anointed by a preacher/pastor the opportunity to do so. There are so many people in your city who has never been invited to the church because of shame and guilt of having a child out of wedlock or just never being invited, and this becomes a great moment to extend the love of the church.

Steps of Implementation

1. Involve the members of your congregation by having them contact people they know who are not involved in a church ministry to this worship service to pray for their children.
2. Advertise in the local newspaper and on the radio informing the community of the worship, and have the process of registration for participants organized when they arrive or have participants RSVP.
3. Have a worship service that is non-judgmental but inspirational, and then offer a time for parents to bring their children forward for prayer. Pray for protection, success, good health, educational success, and for their calling to come forth in their life.
4. Have missionaries baby bassinets and other care packages for every participant.

5. Obtain each participants name and information and do your evangelistic follow up shortly after the service with the hope your love will lead them to accept Christ.

EXPECTED OUTCOME

For babies to be all over the place and for the church to be seen as a station of love.

EXPECTED CHALLENGES

For the traditionalist to not understand blessing babies born out of wedlock. It is not the church's job to blame the child and have the child live a life never being prayed over. Keep everybody focused on the real mission of Christ.

CREATIVITY IN WORSHIP

Dr. M. Keith McDaniel Sr.
Macedonia Baptist Church,
Spartanburg, South Carolina
"An Encounter with Jesus"

~John 4:21

"Jesus saith unto her, Woman, believe me, the hour cometh, when ye shall neither in this mountain, nor yet at Jerusalem, worship the Father."

This text finds Jesus and his disciples leaving Judea and traveling toward Galilee. As they traveled toward Galilee, the Bible says he needed to go through Samaria. Upon entering into the region of Samaria, the Bible says Jesus grew tired in his journey, and sat on a well. John, the writer of this text, is careful to note the time. It is the sixth hour or 12 o'clock noon when Jesus sits at the well. It is the middle of the day. Jesus is tired and hungry. His disciples have gone into the city to buy food, while Jesus sat at the well, Jacob's well, and rested.

As He sat, gathering his strength to continue the journey, a woman of the city approached Him, ready to draw water from the same well. Little did she know that her life was about to change. She did not know it, but heaven had navigated her in a most unusual way, for an unusual encounter, with an unusual man, all of which centered on worship in an unusual place.

It is necessary for us to know that heaven majors in the unusual. God specializes in doing the strange thing.

It is necessary for us to know that heaven majors in the unusual. God specializes in doing the strange thing. What seems odd to us, often times is God's chosen path toward the encounter of a lifetime. There is something about Jesus, that when you meet him, He will change your life forever. That is somebody's testimony, when you met Jesus your life changed. You know it changed because you no longer fit where you used to fit. You no longer think how you used to think and you no longer behave how you used to behave. You may not be what you want to be but you are glad you are not what you used to be.

What strikes me about the text is that this woman does not meet Jesus in church or the synagogue. She meets Him at a well in the community. It is critical that we understand this because, all too often we have limited our expression of worship to the building we have come to know as the church. We come to this place, built of brick and mortar, with an expectation to meet God here. Yet there are times when the encounter which changes our lives does not happen within these walls, but somewhere outside of them. Therefore, our expectation of the encounter with God must be expanded to include anywhere and any time.

God is not limited. God is not limited to the church building. God is not limited to 10:45am Sunday morning. God is not limited to the address or the denomination at the end of a church's name. God is not limited to the number of people that show up or don't show up. God is an omnipresent being, meaning He is in all places at all times. That means I don't have to wait until Sunday morning to have an encounter with God. I don't have to wait until I reach a certain location, such as the church building to worship God. I don't have to wait until Sunday morning to open my Bible. I don't have to wait until Sunday morning to pray and talk to God. Because every day is a day of thanksgiving.

An encounter with God is the starting point for true worship! Worship, my dear friends, is fundamentally about God. It is our attempt to express the value we have placed on God. What God means to us, the importance of God's role in our lives, the significance of the Savior should be evident in our worship. Worship is what we offer to God, not so much because of what He does for us, but rather because of whom He is to us. He is the one who gives us life, liberty and loves us more than we love ourselves. He is the one who made us in His own image. He is the one who started the love affair between Heaven and Earth. We love Him because He loved us first. Worship is fundamentally about God. Yet, worship is not limited to a particular place or a particular setting or a particular time.

Worship should not be so routine it becomes predictable, but every now and then there ought to be something unusual about worship. There ought to be some moments in our lives when we worship God outside the walls of this church. There ought to be some moments in our lives when we are walking around in our own homes worshiping God. There ought to be some moments on your job when you find yourself in worship. Even while driving in your car it is possible to break out in worship.

The Bible says in verse 19 of text the woman perceived Jesus was a prophet. Upon her perception of Jesus, she raised a theological question, concerning the location of Worship. She said unto him, "Our fathers worshipped on this mountain; and ye say, that in Jerusalem is the place where men ought to worship." Jesus responds to her by saying, "Woman, believe me, the hour cometh, when ye shall neither in this mountain, nor yet at Jerusalem, worship the Father." In other words, she believed Mt. Gerizim was the place of worship. Jacob's well was there and it was viewed as one of the holy places on the region. She placed worship at a fixed location. She further argued the Jewish people had another fixed location of worship namely, Jerusalem, the city of David. She believed worship was only possible at a certain fixed location. Jesus' response to her shattered her understanding that both locations were the only places of worship. He said, "the day is coming when worship of the father will not be limited to location." Might I say that that day is now?

He then adds saying in verse 23, "the hour has come and now is, when the true worshippers shall worship the Father in spirit and in truth: for the Father seeketh such to worship him." To seeketh means God is moving. He is searching for someone to worship Him in an unusual way, in an unusual setting. He is looking and searching for the unusual because there is something unusual God wants to do within the confines of the usual. There is something strange God wants to do to the standard. There is a change God wants to bring into the custom. There is spirit God wants to interject into the natural. There is something extra God wants to add to the ordinary.

God is saying to somebody, "I'm getting ready to interrupt your normal routine. I'm getting ready to interrupt the way you have been doing things." God is saying to somebody, "you are getting ready to have an encounter with me that was not on your calendar. It is not on your schedule for the day. It is not in your plans." There are moments when we encounter Jesus outside the walls of the church building.

That is precisely what is happening in this text. This woman's life changed because she had an encounter with Jesus outside the walls of the church. She was going about her day. She had no plans of religious discourse. She had no intention of being converted. She was going through her normal routine, yet she met the Lord in a usual way and her life was forever changed. This woman does not meet the Lord in Church, but she meets Him in the community. The encounter that changes her life does not happen inside the walls of the sanctuary. It happens outside, in the community. I want to examine this text to understand the theology of worship outside the usual locations, outside the walls of this building. What made this moment so impactful to her life?

The first thing I noticed about this encounter is the encounter was possible because she was not watching the clock. One of the fundamental problems with worship inside the sanctuary is we are constantly watching the clock. The encounter with Jesus and this woman took place because a usual task took place at an unusual time. I know that because drawing water was a familiar task for the women in the community, but drawing water alone at the 6th hour or noon was unusual. Most women drew water together, in groups at the cool hours of the morning or later in the evening when the Sun was descending. Drawing water was a community action of the women. They did this together.

Yet, the text says this woman does not have a crowd with her, nor has she come at the usual time, but has she come at the 6th hour, high noon, the hottest point in the day to draw water. So here she is, by herself, she has missed the crowd. She is coming at an unusual time, to do a usual task. It is not normal to draw water from a well at noon. You draw water from a well in the morning or in the evening. Yet, despite the fact it was not the normal time to draw water did not negate the fact the woman needed the water. So her placement at the well was not according to time, but according to need.

The problem with limiting our experience of worship to the church building, is the fact that if we only worship God here...

The problem with limiting our experience of worship to the church building, is the fact that if we only worship God here, we become religious clock-watchers, instead of relational God watchers! Yet, the true worshipers in the room can relate to this because there are times when God will have you doing a normal task at an unusual time, but the task is not based on the time but based on the need. I have found out that when I need something from God it does not matter what time is on the clock. When I need something from God, I do not worry about the time. My focus is on God! Have you ever found yourself praying to God at 2:30 in the morning? It wasn't your normal prayer time but you needed to talk to Him. The task of prayer was not limited to time but based upon your need.

The woman came to the well at noon because of her need for water. God is looking for a people who are no longer looking at the clock but are willing to keep their eyes on Jesus! Too many times we miss the encounter with God because we are watching the clock. We have made the mistake to limit worship to a particular place that starts at a particular time and we are constantly watching the clock when we should be watching Jesus. We come to church on countdown mode! We live our lives on countdown mode! Yet what we failed to realize is everything in our lives does not happen according to our time! Can I tell you something? No amount of clock watching will make God move! No amount of anxiety about the time will add to your life. God is looking for true worshipers, not clock-watchers!

The encounter with Jesus was made possible because she was not watching the clock. Secondly, this encounter was made possible because Jesus was tired. The text says Jesus needed to go through Samaria and upon entering into Samaria the Bible says he grew tired. In verse 6, His fatigue brought Him to the well. Her need for water brought her to the well. There was a limit to Jesus' physical endurance. Because He was wrapped in the flesh, He was subject to things this flesh is subject to and he honored the limit of his flesh. He was tired, and because He was tired He stopped at this well. His physical fatigue in the text, is a manifestation of His spiritual fatigue with us. That is to say, God has grown tired of some things in our lives.

God grows tired of us doing the same things over and over again. God grows tired of us saying we are going to do something and we never do it! God has grown tired of average worship when He has given us all we have. God has grown tired of getting us out of the same situations. God has grown tired of walking with us but we are not walking with him. God has grown tired of worship that does not display the true value of His presence in our lives.

Not only does God grow tired, we should grow tired of some things in our lives. We should be tired of business as usual. We should be tired on doing the same things. We should be tired of coming to church and having good worship in here, but seeing no real and lasting change in the community. Jesus stopped at this well because He was tired.

There are some people who will not come to church because they have grown tired from the journey of life. There are some people who have sat down in the despair of day, who have not progressed past the pain, people who have not moved beyond the burden. There are some people who are unable to move forward. If the church is going to reach them, the church cannot wait for them, the church must meet where they are. That is to say, if they will not come to church, the church must go to wherever they are.

This encounter was possible because the woman was not watching the clock. The encounter was possible because of the fatigue of Jesus. Thirdly, this encounter with Jesus was possible because Jesus was willing to talk and the woman was willing to listen. Jesus came to the well because of His fatigue. The woman came to Jacob's well because of her need for water. The "well" represented for one a place of rest and for the other a place of refreshment. The "well" represented a common place where the two could interact. When we worship God in the common places of our communities, it provides an opportunity for God to change the atmosphere.

Jesus initiates the conversation by asking for something to drink. She response by raising a question. She wants to know why Jesus is talking to her. She is a Samaritan and He is Jew. This is not simply a statement of ethnicity it is also a statement of faith and religion. The Samaritans were a ethno-religious group. The Jews were ethno-religious people. Which means the ethnicity and the religion were extremely connected. She was careful to note Jews are the ones who have not dealings with the Samaritan. One of the reasons why worship outside the walls of the church is necessary is because there are elements within the community that believe the church does not care about them. If the church does not care for them, they may conclude God does not care for them. There are many people who have navigated their whole lives around and beyond the influence of the church. Yet, Jesus initiates the conversation.

The woman is not the one who initiates the conversation. It is Jesus. He makes the request for water. He makes the request to have His need met by her. She hesitates because normally people who look like Jesus do not speak to her. It was George G. Hunter III who wrote, "The vast majority of churches have not, within memory, reached and discipled any really secular persons! Many churches would be astonished if it ever happened, because many churches do not even intend to reach lost people outside their church's present circle of influence. Their main business is caring for their members." She is not use to church people talking to her. She is used to church people walking pass her without saying a word. Might I say it is an indictment on the church when people refuse to come to church because of the way church people have treated them. Isn't this a shame? Sometimes you have to take worship outside the walls of the church, to show the people on the outside that everybody inside is not all bad.

Jesus starts the conversation with this woman. He initiates connect. He sought her out and gave her the opportunity to meet his need. He recognized her value. He recognized her ability and He talked to her. If the church is going to impact the community for the glory of God, the church must become involved in the community. The worship environment of the church must be relevant at the various wells within our communities. What "wells" in our community does the church need to situation itself? What "wells" within our community desperately need of an encounter with Jesus? What "wells" within our community are trying to survive with their needs being met with temporary resource, when Jesus is ready to offer living water? Why wait for someone to come to church before we introduce them to Jesus Christ? Jesus is ready to meet them at the well of their current location.

CREATIVITY IN MUSIC

Pastor Kurt A. Campbell

Ignite Christian Fellowship

Creedmoor, North Carolina

Throughout the Bible, we observe humankind is admonished to praise God. This is the highest praise. God has given grounds for the name of the LORD to be praised, for the power of God is unsurpassed and the love of God is not equaled. We witness and can attest to the fact humankind receives daily blessings from the LORD. However, when standards are raised and God is praised, we also become the recipients of intangible blessings. Praise from a life of obedience and honor will always result in greater benefits (cf. Deut 28: 1-14). As the LORD is glorified, inner peace, greater than our comprehension, and spiritual rest are imparted to us (cf. Is 26:3; Mt 11: 28-30; Phil 4:6, 7). As blessed creatures, recognizing the Creator's great and marvelous works, we must ultimately come before the LORD with thanksgiving, gladness, and celebration (cf. Ps 100). Moreover, with passion, we must spread the Good News of Jesus Christ, the Savior, and LORD (cf. Mt 28: 16-20). In addition to our obedience and spreading the Gospel, God can also be glorified through the plethora of talents we possess. The capacity to honor and thank the LORD

Imagine rushing waves of water, rain falling into a pond, and leaves rustling in the air as sounds resonating from a percussion section.

with our talents comes solely from what God has granted. Among the talents God has bestowed is the gift of music.

I believe music has been present since creation. Nature is constantly producing the orchestral and choral sounds of a symphony. Imagine rushing waves of water, rain falling into a pond, and leaves rustling in the air as sounds resonating from a percussion section. Picture the call of the elephant, the cries of other land animals, and sea creatures forming the brass section. Capture in your mind's eye the fluting of small birds, the screams of birds of prey, and the quacking of ducks making up the woodwinds. Visualize the high and low buzzing pitches and tones of winged insects constituting stringed instruments. Envision the wind blowing through mountains, caves, and canyons tempering sounds of 'oohs' and 'ahs'. From soft slow rolling sounds of thunder from afar, to the quick attacks of lighting and thunder nearby, imagine the musical expression notations of crescendos, decrescendos, pianissimos, and fortissimos, (representing volume dynamics), the meter and the tempo. Finally, even when there is the moment of silence in the earth, think about the measure of rest, a transition to the next movement, or the ending of a musical composition and an audience responding with a standing ovation. These sounds are just some of the means nature with its multi purposes is designed to give God honor and be an example to humankind.

However, even when nature is at its pinnacle of praise, God, Who gave humankind dominion over the earth, receives our praise above all. Unlike nature, which instinctively praises God, humankind is distinctively created to glorify God by freewill, under his or her own volition. Even more specific, God's children praise the LORD for grace and mercy. Our love of God is reflective of God's love to us (cf. 1Jn 4:19). We magnify the LORD for salvation and deliverance through Jesus Christ. Our hearts are made to rejoice knowing God is near and the Holy Spirit dwells within us. God is pleased when the apex of creation loves and glorifies the LORD with all their heart and strength (cf. Deut. 6:5, Mt 22:37). It is a blessing to have the God-given talent of music. Using all that is within and gleaning from the sounds of nature, we must nurture this talent and use it to honor God.

As we live, is the canvas of life painted with hopes of its completion, or before we are born, is the canvas of life already painted?

Much can be said concerning music and its affect. In nearly every locale of our lives we hear various genres of music. At home, church, school, in automobiles, businesses, shopping centers and malls, restaurants, medical facilities, during parades, sports and social events, we hear music. Musical concerts and plays are also designed for listening enjoyment and enlightenment. When the music is heard, its purpose is to set an atmosphere conducive to the emotional and mental results desired. As seen in the following accounts, joyful music was sung when the children of Israel were delivered by God from the hands of the Egyptians (cf. Ex 14-15). The Lord also being with David, used him to play the harp and refresh Saul of the evil spirit from God troubling him (cf.1Sam 16:14-23). Soft, slow music is generally played or sung to induce calm, while fast loud music often creates or is the result of excitement. Within my mind, these questions arise: Does life imitate art, or is art influenced by life? As we live, is the canvas of life painted with hopes of its completion, or before we are born, is the canvas of life already painted? Furthermore, do we write a song not knowing how it sounds or ends? In answer to these questions, I have no doubt from the beginning the Artist, who is also the Life Giver, inseparably created life and art, and knows it in its fullness. As musicians make melodious sounds from the wonderful gift of life and art, it should be with all intent to glorify God. Since we are impacted by the power of music, Christians should discover methods to use the diverse genres of music as instruments for God's glory. Keeping an open mind enables us to use everything at our disposal for Kingdom building.

To speak of art as it relates to life, we must understand the perception of an artist. An artist may be determined to hone his or her skills one dimensionally, narrowing the focus, limiting imagination, allowing no room for error of thought. Alternatively, an artist may soar far beyond one's immediate thought and tap into an endless realm of possibilities. Abstract, impressionistic, avant-garde, ad-lib, and improvisational arts are derivatives of this thought process. Likewise, in photography, the same pattern is considered. Photographers "zoom in" with a camera lens to give definition and detail of a specific person or object as the primary subject. They also "zoom out" to display a panoramic scene, or a scene with an unlimited view. Nevertheless, whether zooming in or panning out, both the artist and photographer never stray from the aspiring theme. These illustrations are disclosed to demonstrate it should unequivocally be the same in relation to Christ and our commission from Him to evangelize.

To live a God centered life and never lose base, similar to artists and photographers, Christians must both "zoom in" and "pan out" on Christ. During Hampton University's Ninety-First Minister's Conference, in a lecture entitled "The Theology of Balance" Dr. Robert Smith, Jr., urged those who carry the gospel of Jesus Christ to give diligence to following the basic rule applied in music composition by returning to the "tonic." The tonic signifies the keynote of a musical composition. Often heard at the beginning of music is the tonic note or the tonic chord. When the tonic is heard, little doubt is raised of it being the main note in the music. Throughout a composition, movements and variations of the theme artic-ulate a grand design panning out for a wider view; however, the tonic is the composition's strength. Returning to the tonic denotes concreteness and finality, defining, without question, the theme of the composition. Dr. Smith emphasized there should be a return to the soundness of the Scripture and spiritual roots, focusing on the complete Word of God. Concentration on the Word in its fullness is paramount to widening tunnel vision, defusing unfounded dogma, and censuring skepticism. It may be rather simple to form an opinion of Christ based upon church protocol. However, to gain a better point of view, Christians must also "pan out" and look from other angles at Christ. This entails recognizing Christ in relationship to the world and not only the Church.

The first genre of music I choose to discuss is religious music or church music. This music is set to give glory and honor to God. Additionally, it offers assurance of God's power, stimulates our faith, confers upon the worshipers a sense of devotion and commitment, consoles the weary and downtrodden; and invites sinners to repentance. If much of this sounds similar to preaching, it is because it compliments, agrees, and promotes the Word in the form of song and or musical instrumentation. Initiated with a sincere heart, and a high standard of skill from practice, it will ultimately glorify God. I considered using Paul's letter to the Church at Ephesus as an example to encourage music ministries. Paul prays "That Christ may dwell in your hearts by faith; that ye, being rooted and grounded in love, may be able to comprehend with all saints what is the breadth, length, and depth, and height; and to know the love of Christ...." (Eph 3 17-19a KJV). These words speak volumes to the growth and expansion of music ministry. The challenge is to juxtapose Paul's writing of dimensions to music ministry. "Breadth" or width, which also refers to thickness or mass, indicates the music is solid and totes a message of truth. "Length," carrying the notion of distance and duration, denotes its longevity, completion, and efficient delivery. "Depth" implies the music is relevant to the subject and makes sense. This would constitute the message as being deep. It can be achieved with or without many words. "Height," which is the last dimension mentioned, indicates a lifting of the spirit through encouragement. Combined, it is the power of God's love through Jesus Christ working in the music. The ministry should constantly observe rendering music with these dimensions.

Conversely, non-religious music is the second form of music I wish to discuss. I chose to use the word non-religious instead of secular. The term "secular" is far more demeaning, for it indicates worldliness and opposition to religion and faith. Therefore, it should be noted, not all non-religious music falls into the category of secularism. A vast amount of music not heard in the Church inspires, encourages, and spawns creativity. Some Christians tend to accept religious or Christian music only, labeling other forms of music as "secular" and sinful. Some also choose to live a life of seclusion, refraining from many of the pleasures God intended for us to enjoy. Others are selective, accepting and rejecting some non-religious music. For example, classical music is widely accepted but jazz has little acceptance. For many who react this way to music, their choice is based on their interpretation of passages in the Bible. Three passages commonly used to support their claims are Ex 32:1-20, Amos 6:5, and 2Cor 6:14-17. I neither commend nor condemn this stance. However, after careful examination of these passages, I conclude the LORD was standing and speaking against the perverseness of idolatry and unbelief. The vile music expressed the condition of their hearts, but it was not the culprit of their sin.

I firmly believe God intended for men and women to have many pleasures beyond the Church. Led by the Word and the Spirit of God, sons and daughters of God have power to enjoy life without falling into degradation, debauchery, and disgrace. Personally, I love Church music; however, it is not the only music I engage myself in hearing. I enjoy listening to many types of music. This amazing gift is filled with many talented people who cover a wide range of music. The genres of music I listen include but are not limited to gospel music, jazz, classical, rhythm and blues, country, rock, and hip-hop. Although, I listen to these forms of music, I do not accept everything I hear. I pay special attention to lyrics and reject music promoting idolatry, self-indulgence, degrading gender, and bigotry. Otherwise, I receive music for its artistry, originality, and delight. I have attended gospel, jazz, classical, country, rhythm and blues, and rock concerts. As a musician, I have played in many of the same. I am filled with joy when I hear powerful singers and musicians render gospel music. However, I also enjoy hearing the instrumentation of classical compositions. It often has me on the edge of my seat. Jazz music takes my breath away as I wonder how such creative improvisation is expressed. I am often caught tapping my foot to the beat of rhythm and blues music. Country music calms me with its simplicity and down-to-earth style. Hip-hop artists astonish me at their rapid rhyming lyrics. I challenge myself with little success to rhyme as fast as they do. Moreover, I especially enjoy listening to love ballads music when I am with my wife. Much of what I am thinking is said through music. Many may denounce me as a hypocrite or a backslider.

It is very difficult to engage in conversation when you have little or no clue of how people live.

However, I am firmly rooted in the Word of God. My faith is contingent upon my trust in God and my actions to others. To step out and evangelize to men and women not exposed or committed to what is practiced in the Church, Christians should be aware of what occurs outside the Church. During his ministry, Jesus ministered to those outside the places of worship. Christians must learn what is taking place in the world to speak to life's issues, or we will be powerless and offensive in our efforts to evangelize Christ. It is very difficult to engage in conversation when you have little or no clue of how people live. Evangelism requires us to be harmless as doves and cunning as serpents (cf.

Mt 10:16). Therefore, we must study the practices of those we attempt to reach. In error, many who wish to evangelize expect the world to be like the Church. To their surprise and dismay, they quickly find out differently. Using church vernacular is a turn-off to those outside the Church. Evangelism involves moving past the borders of the Church with secured faith to a world of diversity. When we depart the church premises, we hear less music of the Church. Whether or not we accept non-religious music, we should consider it as an instrument for winning souls. Music is often art influenced by life. The LORD is the Giver of life and music; and as I stated previously, it is all to glorify God. Therefore, we must take what God has given and construct it in a manner to reach the lost. To "pan out" and yet remain focused on the theme, we must speak of music and its effects, its relation to life, while cleverly pointing the way to Christ. It is imperative to choose the appropriate conversation for each group and individual. If you have little knowledge or experience of a subject, allow someone who is knowledgeable to lead in conversation while you listen closely.

When applying music as a tool for evangelism, use metaphors for impact. With classical music, cite how the conductor has control, eventually assuring that God is in control. For jazz, make a note of the soloist improvising in an augmented key, stating God is able to augment or raise our minds above situations and circumstances beyond our power. Relative to rhythm and blues, drive in the thought God is steady and never misses a beat. For country music and its simplicity, talk of God's power to give peace and serenity. For hip-hop and its rhyming expressions of life, poetically speak of the joy received living for God. Incorporate relevant and positive non-religious music lyrics into sermons. It will be something persons who know very little of the Bible will understand. I also suggest carefully planned concerts sponsored by the church as an outreach vehicle. Employ people with an outstanding reputation and good character to undergird this task. Don't be afraid to attend concerts with individuals who have not accepted Christ. However, make sure you remain committed to the cause. Your willingness to be with them is encouraging. In addition, mention the wonderful non-religious songs that are God inspired like "Lean On Me" by Bill Withers, "Man In The Mirror" by Michael Jackson, "I Look To You" by Robert Kelly and sung by Whitney Houston, to name a few. Finally, use the music that is truly secular as a topic of dialogue for change, self-worth, and life preservation, converting the negative message to a positive one. Be creative. I recall using in a sermon the acronyms "C.R.E.A.M." meaning "cash rules everything around me" from a hip-hop group called the "Wu Tang Clan." Using the same acronyms, preaching on the superiority of our LORD, I changed its meaning to "Christ rules everything around me." To accomplish God's purpose, what is meant for evil, the LORD is able to change for good (cf. Gen 50:21). Once the heart and mind are conditioned, through the Spirit of God, I believe souls will come to Christ. You will experience the awesome power of God when you "pan out" and "zoom in" on Christ as the theme, and returning to Him as the "Tonic."

In conclusion, all of the sounds of nature replicated by humankind will return to the Artist. From the beginning, the painting and song were complete. The Artist and Life Giver, who is the Almighty God, never lost glory. God's plan is that we who are lost might be found, and by the power of the Holy Spirit be saved by grace through faith in looking to Jesus Christ, the Lamb of God who takes away the sin of the world (cf. Lk 15; Eph 2:5; Jn 1: 29). In the place called Heaven, the redeemed of the LORD are given authority to use the peak of nature's sounds. The music heard at the beginning will come full circle; however, instead of it being through nature, it will be through the saints. The Apostle John said "And I heard as it were the voice of a great multitude, and as the voice of many waters, and as the voice of mighty thunderings, saying 'Alleluia: for the Lord God Omnipotent reigneth'." (Rev 19:6 KJV) O, what a blessing and honor to be there, possessing the original sounds of music, forever praising God! Amen.

THE CREATIVITY OF REACHING YOUNG FATHERLESS MALES

Dr. John Tyus

ID Movement

Columbus, Ohio

The young black male struggles for self-identity in a culture that tries to give them everything else but what they truly need. Self-identification is one of the single most important factors in a man's life to discover. Self-discovery is what everyone is looking for in some form. A strong parental foundation has been proven to be key factors in aiding children find themselves. Parents being the first example of humanity that a child sees, they have an overwhelming responsibility to showcase what children can expect to become. Self-awareness is built from whatever foundation a child is given, that foundation being parents they are the springboard to what the child will become. "Train up a child in the way he should go, even when he is old he will not depart from it" (Proverbs 22:6, ASV) If the child is trained up correctly according to their gifting and calling, they will grow older and won't depart from their upbringing and their lives will become fruitful. This is important because this shines the light on the importance of parents making sure they train their children up properly. The fathers must be present to provide a foundation for their children and must live what they teach in their homes. It falls back on the parents in showing their children their purpose. King Solomon emphasizes the importance of the parents knowing their children's destinies and their personalities and knowing how to mold and shape them into who they were destined to become in life. In order for the parents to know and understand the gifts and calling of the children, they must 1) spend much time learning and studying the child and 2) seek God for guidance on how to mold, shape, and cultivate them into who they are to become. Helping the children learn their gifting is an essential factor in helping them find their purpose. Once the gift is found, there lies their place of service, fulfillment, and purpose. Parents are to know their children's purpose or at least place of gifting before the child does.

It is fathers that are the foundation of the family, without a proper foundation any building will collapse.

It is fathers that are the foundation of the family, without a proper foundation any building will collapse. It is crucial for the male to be present in the child's life. If not the child needs a male figure or mentor to aid in the development process. National Fatherhood Initiative which was founded in 1994 by Don Eberly, a former White House advisor, met with other scholars to address a growing issue which was absent fathers in our communities. National Fatherhood Initiative was birthed to help the issue of father absentee. On their website they state, "According to the U.S. Census Bureau, 24 million children in America — one out of three – live in biological father-absent homes. Consequently, there is a father factor in nearly all of the social issues facing America today."[1] Eberly started this foundation on these 4 principles issues,

---

[1] "Statistics and Data on the Consequences of Father Absence." Fatherhood.org. http://www.fatherhood.org/about/organization-history (accessed July 1, 2013).

1) Father makes unique and irreplaceable contributions to the lives of children. 2) Father absence produces negative outcomes for children, 3) Societies which fail to reinforce a culture ideal of responsible fatherhood get increasing amounts of father absence, 4) Widespread fatherlessness is the most socially consequential problem of our time.[2]

Can these fatherlessness issues be solved through spiritual healing? Men without a proper model lack stability and wholeness, Dr. Howard Thurman refers to this in his theology of human liberation. Men without a proper model in their lives are faced with inward fears that prevent them from facing life's responsibilities and that fear encourages them to try to solve the issue in negative ways and attach themselves to negative people. Christ came to heal us from fears and abandonment issues, bringing forth wholeness within our emotions and mentally. He covers our lack and solidifies who we are and brings forth self-realization. Thurman states, "Wherever Jesus spirit appears, the oppressed gather fresh courage; for He announced the good news that fear, hypocrisy, and hatred the three hounds of hell that tract the trail of the disinherited, need to have no dominion over them."[3] This provides hope for those that are broken by their lack of representation from fathers within their lives. While mentors can help, ultimately it is God who will provide direction. They lack wholeness and feel a need for affirmation.

"Wherever Jesus spirit appears, the oppressed gather fresh courage; for He announced the good news that fear, hypocrisy, and hatred the three hounds of hell that tract the trail of the disinherited, need to have no dominion over them."

---

[2] Ibid.

One must look at the Bible and its ideals concerning its look on fathering from a biblical perspective. "But above all, fathers in Israel became teachers of their children, not primarily in that more sophisticated mode exhibited in the book of Proverbs but through daily contact and informal conversations between themselves and their children (Dt 11:19), prompted more often than not by questions posed by the children themselves."[4] Without teaching the children are left to teach themselves and go through life missing foundational truths that were never instilled by their father, causing lack within their lives.

This oppression can be healed and liberated by Christ, which Thurman speaks about. Males that grow up without a proper male model in their lives are faced with adversity inwardly and lack within themselves, a need for affirmation, and a lack of wholeness. Christ came to liberate those who are broken and lack completeness; this is applicable to this sect of individuals. It is only through Christ like Thurman states that man can realize self-actualization. It is impossible to know who you are until you know where you have come from. Christ used a mentoring model on his disciples, as did Paul with Timothy, Paul with Titus, Moses with Joshua, and countless others. It was through successors that the mentor themselves were able to live on.

Jawanza Kunjufu further touches on this by stating "Unfortunately, if there's an absent of fathers, crime increases. We have too many boys with guns primarily because we have too few fathers in the home. Crime increases in neighborhoods without fathers because neighborhoods

---

[3] Alonzo Johnson, *Good News for the Disinherited: Howard Thurman on Jesus of Nazareth and Human Liberation* (New York: University Press of America, 1997), 95.

[4] John W. Miller, *Calling God Father: Essays on the Bible Fatherhood & Culture* (New York: Paulist Press, 1999), 93.

without men able and willing to confront youth, chase threatening gangs and reproach delinquent fathers are at risk."[5]

From this issue of fatherlessnes, The I.D. Movement was created which focuses on mentoring young fatherless men from the ages of 12-18. The project discovered that when young men that have grown up without a father figure in their lives are mentored through simple life principles there is a change in their attitudes, communication with their mothers, and they experience more self-awareness concerning fatherhood/men and they have a better chance of connecting to God. These sessions helped the young men deal with their pain and help discover a form of healing through expression, which in effect aids them as men, and positively affecting their families, communities, and lives. While immediate change in many ways will not be seen, it is a seed planted in the lives of these young men and its effects will sprout over time. All sessions were facilitated or co-facilitated by myself. The interesting addition to the program was that each session was held at a different location each week in the presence of the co-facilitator, which was a positive male figure, giving the young men experimental learning. They not only heard the stories of positive males but they were able to see the stories of positive males. Topics that were discussed was forgiveness with your father, conflict management, discovering your pain, passion and purpose, the importance of education, God the father, honoring and respecting women, biblical family structure and dressing like a prospect instead of a suspect.

This project's aim is to empower and cultivate a sense of belonging for young fatherless black males using interactive teachings that will foster a sense of pride and consciousness as a male. This model assisted the young men in identifying their gifting and pointed them in the direction of their

---

[5] Jawanza Kunjufu, *Restoring The Village: Solutions For The Black Family* (Chicago, IL: African American Images, 2003), 31.

maker, God. The teaching was interactive and pulled from a host of issues and topics that young men can relate to. Using current ways of communication such as Facebook was utilized to further communicate positive messages weekly to the young males. The model consisted of young males from the ages of twelve to eighteen that have not had a substantial father figure in their lives and that were being raised by single mothers or grandparents. The young men came from various relations from my context such as basketball team members of one of the men at our church, young men that have been adopted into families affiliated with World Conquerors through Jesus Christ. Through this project, student's awareness concerning the importance of fathers and themselves increased. The data triangulation used for this project include: Pre-assessment, post-assessment, participant-interviews, and parent-interviews. Each session was filmed along with interviews of the young men involved for the purposes of creating a documentary for the community.

CREATIVE YOUTH MINISTRY

Dr. Kia R. Hood, Site Pastor

Union Baptist Church-Jamestown/High Point, North Carolina

The fundamental purpose of this lecture is to consider a few concepts that can help us develop a culture for effective youth ministry in the 21st Century. The idea of having an effective youth ministry has been an evolving concept for decades. With a culture that is captivated by Love and Hip Hop Atlanta, World Star, and other challenging popular shows that glorifies violence, sex, and unhealthy relationships, the church must be intentional how they reach children and youth. We are competing against the age of Twitter, Facebook, Instagram, SnapChat, and YouTube. We are at war with iPhones, iPads, Internet and technology. There is an epidemic of suicide, gun violence, unlawful incarceration, and policy brutality among our youth. The U.S. pregnancy rate has dropped 9%, still, the U.S. teen pregnancy rate is substantially higher than in other western industrialized

If the church limits its efforts of building and effective youth ministry, we face the possibility of losing our youth to gangs, alternative religious practices, or completely denouncing the Christian faith.

nations, and racial/ethnic and geographic disparities in teen birth rates persist, according to the Center for Disease Control report.

If the church limits its efforts of building and effective youth ministry, we face the possibility of losing our youth to gangs, alternative religious practices, or completely denouncing the Christian faith. Youth Ministry is important and vital to the development of the church and community. If we are to be the church that believes in revival and renewal, let us consider how we can revive our youth ministry to be whole, relational and effective. Youth Ministry can be challenging and rewarding. However, effective youth ministry is necessary for not only for the lifeline of our ministries, but also for the development of our community.

Biblical View of the Value of Youth - In Matthew 19: 1 -15, we find a very interesting conversation that Jesus is having with the Pharisees. They are challenging Jesus on the topic of divorce and if it is lawful. Jesus refers them to consider when God joins people together, let no one separate. Jesus gives the law of Moses, explains the papers or documents of divorce and as He is talking, there appears to be a small youth group that arrive to see Him. They come to get the blessings of Christ. Yet, the disciples become hostile and try to push them away. Jesus tells them to bring the children to Him so that he may lay hands on them and that the Kingdom belongs to them also.

What is interesting about this text is the immediate connection that Jesus has with the children. As children are common in these towns and villages, they are considered at a lower standard in hierarchy. However, Jesus takes what is considered "low" and paralles it with the Kingdom of God. As the disciples are pushing them away from the church, Jesus is calling them to Him. A call for anointing/laying of the hands is performed. This sign of ordination gives indication of Jesus's approval of children and their place in the life of the church. He proceeds to give them what they came for, and that is approval and prayer and touch from the Kingdom.

This periscope provides a wide scope for youth ministry. First, we must understand that children belong to the church. When we develop a sternness to push them out by not providing relevant programs, financial support, or not making them a priority, we forbid them for what is rightfully theirs, that is the Kingdom of God. Secondly, the beginning of the text said that they were bought to Jesus. In other words, the parents knew how important it was to get to the church. Rather them stay home and miss the youth conference, choir rehearsal, Bible study, parents took the time and bought them to Jesus. When was the last time, we bought youth/children to Jesus? Have we allowed them to miss their blessings because they wanted to stay home or not attend events and small groups? When they arrive, Jesus did not dismiss them, but he blessed them.

Jesus understood the value of youth and what they had to offer to the Kingdom of God. When our churches adopt the Jesus method of handling youth, we will find our youth ministries growing spiritually. Don't shew them away, the Kingdom belongs to them. When we closely exam this text, it reminds us that we must not forsake the assignment and purpose of youth. They are important and according to Jesus, the Kingdom belongs to them. Therefore, youth ministries across the globe must align with Christ's vision for children... bring them to the church for that is where they belong. The challenge for youth ministries is when they come, what will you give them?

Common Challenges of Youth Ministry

Let us face it, youth ministry can be fun, but it also presents a few challenges. As we try to develop effective youth ministries, many deal with road blocks that hinder us from developing effective youth ministries.

Challenge 1 – Lack of Vision and Goal Setting: Great ideas are important, but a great idea without a vision and goal setting will turn into a nightmare. Vision and goal setting is important. It allows youth leaders to understand the "big picture" or what your youth ministry goals and accomplishments are. Your vision and goal is the road map to a successful youth ministry. Lay out the vision for your youth ministry each year. Establish obtainable goals that meet the overall needs for your youth ministry. In developing your goals, be sure to share the vision with your pastor, youth workers, youth and parents. The issue with a vision that is not shared is that it becomes a guessing game to those who should be a part. Therefore, the aim of effective youth ministry to set your goals and be sure they are obtainable. In addition, share the vision with others and cast it so that they may run with it. In your goal setting efforts, be sure that your vision is not copied from someone else. It is easy to Google other youth ministries and mimic their goals, missions, etc. The problem with that is those visions and goals are designed for that culture, youth ministry or community. Find the need in your own community and set your vision and goals on their needs and execute it! Don't be afraid to be who God has designed you to be.... this can be defined as AUTHENCITY of Youth Ministry!

Challenge 2 -Lack of Parental Support: In my experience, I have learned that parents are an essential component to youth ministry. Remember, most youth cannot get to small groups, Bible Study, outings, or other youth events without their parents. Lack of parent support is common, however they must be involved in the process. Parents tend to see youth ministry as a "glorified babysitting service." It is seen as physical deposit for someone else to handle, rather than an opportunity for spiritual growth and development. In result, parents do not become spiritually or personally invested in their child's spiritual growth. To counteract this, I would like to recommend providing a strong parent support group quarterly where youth workers go over calendar events, discuss upcoming small group discussion, introduce new youth workers, discuss the importance of their child being involved. It would also be great to provide a calendar of events that is projected for six months. This allows parents to see what's coming up and to plan accordingly.

Challenge 3 – The Recycle of Faithful Youth Workers: In youth ministry, we tend to see the same youth workers doing the work. It becomes a challenge to get new workers to volunteer and support youth ministry. One thing that I have learned is that youth ministry is not the most glorified ministry in the church. When you have to deal with moody teenagers, hormonal middle schoolers, anxious children and noninvolved parents that is enough reason not to want to participate in youth ministry. However, youth ministry has to be a passion and for most youth workers they stay in it because they understand the outcome of doing effective youth ministry. It is that very moment when that youth has had challenges with their spiritual growth and suddenly you start to see them lead devotion, show signs of leadership and servitude. Those are the moments that we live for. It's the moments like Jeremiah's call when they realize that God has truly ordained them to do the work.

For this challenge, always look for opportunity to recruit people who have heart for youth and who are safe as it pertains to working with youth. There are people in your congregations and communities that are just waiting for you to approach them and ask them for help. In my experience, I have learned that by simply asking people to help in youth ministry, unleashes a new passion and purpose for themselves. Lastly, be sure to provide ongoing training and meetings for your youth workers. This provides a fertile breeding ground for fresh ideas and opportunities to hear different ways to do youth ministries.

5 Basic Principles of Creative Youth Ministries

Youth ministry has to be creative. If you are to reach this generation.

Youth ministry has to be creative! If you are to reach this generation, consider a few approaches that will help grasp an understanding of effective youth ministry. For many, our youth ministry has become stuck or stale. Our efforts lack the creativity mode that will allow us to not think outside of the box. Now this term "outside of the box" has been used by many, but I would like for us to not think outside of the box, but how do you draw your own shape? It is the box that keeps us confined, but if we begin to draw our own shape, there is a bigger and broader picture that will develop. By drawing your own shape, you create space that allows your vision to move beyond a "box" and now it becomes a shape that only your youth ministry can grow and develop from.

PRINCIPLE 1 – KNOW THE YOUTH CULTURE: I am amazed how many youth workers work with youth, but are discounted from the youth culture. A part of being effective and relevant is understanding what students are dealing with on a daily basis. It is important to know what the latest trends, songs, celebrity highlights, slang, etc. Let's be clear, I am not suggesting that you must use these outlets, however I am suggesting that the knowledge of these will help you connect better with your students. For example, recently, there was a repetition battle between two popular female rap artists, Remi Ma and Nicki Minaj. In a heated rap battle, both artists attempted to upstage the other through explicit lyrics and the reveal of personal matters all in the name of protecting their own identity. Now, as overly unequivocal the lyrics were, I listened and was able to apply it to a discussion with youth about conflict resolution.

The most important thing is that we must understand the culture and world in which students are living. They live in a culture where Twitter is the teacher, Instagram is about validating, Snap Chat is a temporary fix and Facebook is where their future holds. As youth workers, there must be a clear understanding that social media is not disappearing, but rather it is developing into a more complex concept. An effective youth ministry is connected to these avenues and understands the relevancy and ministry use of these avenues will result in reaching and revelation for your youth ministry. In this sense, youth ministry has to be flexible and interchangeable. I like to suggest that you do not write youth ministry in pen because it is too permanent, but rather write it in pencil, so you can erase and be prepared for the every changing youth ministry culture.

PRINCIPLE 2 – AUTHENTIC STUDENT RELATIONSHIPS - A major part of youth ministry is developing effective and appropriate relationships. These relationships must foster growth and development, but most of all it should move students towards a relationship with Christ. Besides great programs and life changing small groups, students come searching for authentic relationships with other students and especially youth workers. It is very important that the youth workers are genuine and understand the sacredness of "safe spaces." Students want to know that when they come to a youth worker that the space will be free of judgment, misinterpretation, and will be kept confidential. In this, the youth worker must be aware that if a student is presenting signs of hurting themselves or others, you must act ethically and report this type of behavior. However, if it is that a student is dealing with self-esteem, sexuality concerns, or just need to vent about their parents, they need to know that what they say will not leave the confinements of their conversation. The moment that you abuse a student's trust, you damage that relationship and the relationship with other students. Therefore, the job of the youth worker is to provide a place of authentic relationship that are spiritual and appropriate.

PRINCIPLE 3 – YOUTH INVOLVEMENT IN PLANNING AND DEVELOPING YOUTH MINISTRY – Students like to belong and sense that they are a part of the big picture. Give your students ownership of youth ministry. When you involve students in the planning and development of youth ministry, they become personally invested. In a conversation with my sister, she brings a great analogy about getting people involved. She mentions that we need to be more than members. Membership is common and everyone can get it. When you think about gym membership, people come and they go. One day you may see them and you may not see them for another 3 – 4 weeks. However, when you are a partner, there is a certain level of investment that you put into it. The aim for youth is not be a member of youth ministry, but rather a partner. You want their input and their involvement. The outcome is to have them personally invested in the youth ministry. When they are invested, they will be committed to aid in its growth. The following are ways to involve youth in your youth ministry:

- Allow students to plan the youth revival or youth conference. Get their input on topics, guest speakers, and themes
- Form a youth council and allow that to be their platform to create new ideas for youth ministry
- Speak and fully participate in Youth Day
- Be a part of the main worship service by participating in various worship components such as the choir, usher ministry, audio and video ministry, security ministry, usher ministry
- Allow them to come to the church during the week to assist with filing, making calls, setting up for small groups, making copies or doing other administrative work.
- Acknowledge their strengths and reshape their areas that need development
- Provide training opportunities for youth to be leaders in the church. Every moment is a teachable moment.

PRINCIPLE 4 – YOUTH MINISTRY PROGRAMS AND EVENTS – The key to structural and effective youth ministry is to provide relevant programs and ministry events for students. The events should be age appropriate and provide a spiritual uplift and encouragement. The challenge with programs and events for many is the absence of a biblical or spiritual foundation. In other words, many plan programs just to plan something. The event has no purpose or biblical foundation. Be careful not to turn your youth ministry into an event or social club. However, if you create and plan programs and events with a meaning, the outcome will result in empowerment, spiritual growth, and personal development.

Age appropriate events and programs are critical to effective youth ministry. Be careful not to combine students for the sake of creating a crowd. Students should participate in discussions and events that center around their issues, concerns and needs. For example, a third grader should not participate in a discussion with 11th graders. Therefore, your ministry programs should center around age and possible gender appropriate dialogue. Remember, the outcome for events and programs is growth and many achieve growth when the environment is conducive for growth. Consider these events and programs for your youth ministry:

- Age appropriate Bible Study/ Small Groups – Consider having themes, movie discussion and connect biblical meanings.
- Develop sports programs – youth love sports and outdoors. Consider forming a church basketball team, football league, baseball, soccer, kick ball tournaments, or volleyball league. Consider joining forces with local churches or YMCA's.
- Youth Conferences and Revivals – Youth enjoy the idea of coming together for a weekend dedicated just for them. Revivals and conference must be anchored in a biblical foundation and centered with an outcome of development and growth for students. Be intentional about guest preachers/speakers. They should provide

a youth centered messages and be relevant. The mistake that many youth ministries make is having speakers/preachers whose message does not relate or connect with students. The dangers of this practice will result in ineffectiveness and the possibility of disconnecting from your main audience, students. In addition, be sure to market your event with youthful marketing tools such as flyers, social media (Instagram, Facebook, Twitter), and announcements in your church and the community. Also, consider advertising on your local hip-hop and R&B station. I know that sounds unorthodox, but remember you are trying to be where people are. Your youth and parents are tuned in to these stations each morning. If you get the attention of the parent, you will have the students.

PRINCIPLE 5 – AN EFFECTIVE YOUTH MINISTRY SHOULD HAVE BIBLICAL FOUNDATION:

At the end of the day, your youth ministry must be anchored in the Word of God. There must be a biblical and spiritual undertone that connects your programs and your students. Let's face it, youth come to church to hang out with their friends, but also many come to find hope for their situations. That is where you come in! Your Bible Studies and events should not just be a social gathering, but it should have a spiritual and biblical foundation. Students should have an understanding of basic biblical foundations; they should be able to connect their life situation to the Bible. For example, if your topic is about bullying, what Bible story or verse would be appropriate for youth? How would you connect this life problem with the Bible? May I suggest, the David and Goliath story. This story is full of imagery and symbolism for youth. Avoid promoting violence and decapitating their bully in literal terms, but rather encourage them that they can face any giant with God's help. The healthy imagery provides hope and allows them to see that giants have weakness and can never harm God's chosen.

Creative Youth Ministry is critical for the life of the church. If ministries want to be intentional about reaching youth, there must be a plan, desire, and team willing to invest in youth ministry. The key is to be consistent and to plan to have a plan and execute the plan with Christ and youth in mind. The outcome is simple, reach youth and empower them to move beyond their circumstances both spiritually and socially. We may not hit every goal or reach every youth, but there should be an attempt to be like Christ and give them what belongs to them... the Kingdom of God!

CREATIVE PASTORAL MENTORING IN THE PRESENT DAY CHURCH

Pastor James H. Wilkes, Jr.
Elon Baptist Church, Elon, North Carolina

John Maxwell once wrote, " Creativity is being able to see what everybody else has seen, what nobody else has thought, so that you can do what nobody else has done." One of the major problems in the body of Christ today, is that we have lost out on our creativity. We have arrived at a place called, "Comfortable" or "Good Enough." It is important to know that the enemy of "Excellence" is "Good Enough." "Good Enough" blocks creativity in our churches and our churches fail.

It is important that we regain our creative mindset back in order for the future of our church to be sustained. However, in order for our churches to become creative, it is important that we seek leaders who have creative visions and ministries. These leaders should then pair themselves with young leaders who will lead our church in the future.

> *It is important that we regain our creative mindset back in order for the future of our church to be sustained.*

A relationship like this would be classified as a mentoring relationship. If the African-American Church does not invest in creative mentoring relationships, the futuristic outlook would be a negative slope. We must find seasoned leaders who have served for numerous years in ministry, and have creative outlooks for their ministries. The goal of this relationship should be for the mentee to eat, sleep, live and breathe creative solutions for the church. Which means this relationship isn't meant to be a weekend relationship, but a lifetime. This relationship should strengthen both the mentor and the mentee. The mentee has the responsibility of listening and watching. The mentor has the responsibility of pouring into the mentee and showing them the rope. The relationship should be a hands-on experience relationship and not just a conversation. While conversation is important but in order to become a creative leader one must take what they learn and put into action.

Their motto should be, "I do, you watch, you do, I watch, We do, We Watch, You do, I'm gone." However, gone doesn't mean that I leave you for good it just means that I trust your ability to sustain our church through creative solutions.

Mentoring relationships have been apart of the development of the church for many years. Dr. Walter Earl Fluker in his book, "Ethical Leadership" records one of the greatest mentoring relationships in American History. This relationship was between Howard Thurman and Martin Luther King Jr. Both of these prestigious men were Morehouse graduates. Thurman states his reasoning for higher education, "We understood that our job was to learn so that we could go back into our communities and teach others." In order for a mentoring relationship to work the mentor must take what he/she has learned, and give it to the mentee who may not have the same opportunities that the mentor had.

Moreover, a mentor must be one who would make an indelible impact in the life of the mentee. Rev. Jesse Jackson talked about the impact of

Thurman as he stated, "we knew it was a blessing to give this prophet a glass of water or to touch the hem of his garment." If we are true to creative mentoring, then the mentor has to be able to reach beyond what the eye can see into the soul and heart of the mentee. However, it is the mentee's job and responsibility to sit at the mentors feet at learn as much as he/she can about creativity. The mentee should never feel that he/she has arrived or that they are the mentor. If the mentee should ever get to this place then the relationship has broken its covenant.

Howard Thurman had people who desired to listen to him because of his integrity and dedication. If the mentoring relationship is to be impactful, the mentor must be one of integrity and dedication.

Furthermore, when King was stabbed in Harlem, it was Thurman who went to encourage him. Not many people know that Thurman went to Harlem to be by King's side. The mentor responsibility is to create a safe space that when the mentee has reached their lowest moments that they can depend on them. There may be times in which the mentee has lost out on their creativity or has a creative block then the mentor should encourage them in ways to get them to start back thinking creative.

I was blessed and fortunate to serve under Bishop Sir Walter L. Mack, Jr. who is one of the most creative persons in America. When I came to him, I had creativity but I had not tapped into it. Serving him allowed me to see what creative ministry is all about. After serving four years with Bishop Mack the Lord blessed me to serve as Senior Pastor of Elon First Baptist Church. Just as King had his lowest moment and Thurman was by his side so was Bishop Mack with me. He had instilled in me the necessary tools to be creative and think outside the box. He encouraged me to have programs that no one else had done or though of before. However, there were times and still are times in which I must rely on Bishop Mack's creativity and wisdom.

If the African-American church is to be successful, it is going to take people like Dr. Thurman and Bishop Mack to invest time and energy in young leaders. It will take people like them who will not get frustrated because we as young leaders don't get it the first time but they continue to work with us. The future of our church looks bright because we have mentors in place who have been successful in creating creative ministry solutions that will be shown to young leaders.

Bishop Mack often tells me, "Son, you're swimming in your own water now" and I often respond, "I may be swimming in my own water, but your still my lifeguard." This kind of relationship is what will sustain our church and our young leaders. I believe there is still hope for creative ministry solutions though our upcoming young leader.

THE CREATIVITY OF MOVING
FROM GOOD TO GREAT

Pastor Kathy Dunton
St. Peters United Methodist Church
Oxford, North Carolina

In *Good to Great,* Jim Collins suggests a number of ways for mediocre companies to move from good to great organizations. Collins' research focuses on what great companies did to become great and sustain their greatness. In addition, Collins adamantly affirms that good is the enemy to great, believing when average companies reconcile that being good is enough, they will never become great thus failing to realize that meritocracy results in ordinary; not greatness. James C. "Jim" Collins author of *Good to Great* gathered research from companies that made the transition from good by looking at: (1) leadership, (2) cumulative stock returns and (3) business practices over a 15-year period. He uses his findings that shows how to take a good organization and turn it into one that produces sustained great results, implementing whatever definition of results best applies to ones' specific organization. Therefore, this summary will discuss what Collins believes is necessary for mediocre companies to become great organizations.

Beginning with what Collins calls Level 5 Leadership which is marked humility, professional will, diligence and ambition for the company, he argues, "true leadership only exists if people follow when they have the freedom not to (Collins 2001)."[6] Since leadership is not tyrannical in nature, competence and discipline character are vital to achieving and maintaining a great organization (Collins 2001). In essence, the right people freely working together keeps the momentum of the organization going in the right direction. The right people are identified as those who: (1) have disciplined thoughts, (2) take disciplined actions and (3) make disciplined decisions.[7] Those displaying a culture of discipline are able to face brutal facts, think discipline thoughts and take discipline actions.

When companies are able to face the hard truths, they are ready to take the necessary steps, moving them in the right direction. Collins introduces the Hedgehog concept as a business and ethical compass for all striving business. The Hedgehog concept encompasses the understanding that "all" organizations both: public and private have opportunities at becoming great if they stay true to these three simple concepts: (1) pursue their passion (2) do what they are best at doing and, (3) only do what drives their economic engine.[8] Leaders of good-to-great companies note, "Anything that does not fit with our Hedgehog Concept, we will not do" (Collins 2001).

In essence, companies trying to become great must be like the hedgehog, concentrating on one thing rather than being like the fox who pursues multiple things. Great leaders identify one thing they are best in the world at doing and they decide how that one thing along with the right people can propel the organization forward to sustained optimal

---

[6] Collins, Jim. Good TO Great. Built to Last

[7] Collins, Jim. Good To Great. Built to Last.

[8] Jim Collins. Good To Great. Built to Last.

outcomes. In conclusion, Collins believes that good companies, whether public or private are capable of becoming great when they have level 5 Leadership and stay true to the hedgehog concept.

Theological Assessment

Jim Collins concluded from research that any organization whether secular or sacred that is willing to take the necessary steps outlined in his Good-to-Great Framework can become great. He further posits that greatness can be attained in the sacred arena by embracing Collins Good-to-Great organizational model.

Great leadership starts with possessing the right character and traits.

Consistent with Collins, great leadership starts with possessing the right character and traits which in turn parallels with Colossians 3:12 stating, "Therefore, as God's chosen people, holy and dearly loved, clothe yourselves with compassion, kindness, humility, gentleness and patience" (NIV). In *Where Have All Our People Gone*, Carl S. Dudley explores the growing trend of church dropouts. Dudley believes that pastoral leadership is playing a pivotal role in declining mainline congregations. However, when there is right character, right leadership and the right people fitting together then, the congregation grows and the church is heading for greatness.[9]

Therefore, leadership in the church, just as in the secular arena begins with the leaders having the right character that drives how they lead people. Consistent with Collins findings, secular leaders influence those they lead just as Jesus influenced his disciples. His disciples were

---

[9] Dudley S. Carl. "Where Have All Our People Gone?" The Pilgrim Press. New York, New York 1979

constantly inquiring what and how they could do things as Jesus did. As leaders of the church, Jesus models the required humility, lowliness, servant-attitude required in Christian leadership today much like what Collins agrees can produce great results in the secular arena.[10]

When leadership rightly identifies and employs others to work in the capacity wherewith they are gifted, then the church can move to doing a great work.

The other key factor that Collins believes moves organizations to greatness is getting the right people on the bus. The question is, how can leadership get the right people on the bus in an endeavor to stimulate the church to greatness? The Scripture teaches, without a vision, the people perish. Hence, the primary task of the Christian leadership is to affirm the gifts, graces and talents of those they lead so that they can function in their God-given talents thus moving the church in its intended direction. Matthew 25: 14-30 reinforces that God gives us talents so that we can grow and multiply, not just for ourselves but for others as well. When leadership rightly identifies and employs others to work in the capacity wherewith they are gifted, then the church can move to doing a great work.

Finally, Collins believes if leadership is dedicated to doing that *one* thing that produces over-the-top results over a sustained time period of then, secular organization can become great. The question for the sacred arena is: what is the *one* thing that will produce excessive results over a long period of time in the church? Paul echoes in 1 Corinthians 13:2: "If

---

[10] Matthew 20: 26-28, "Yet it shall not be so among you; but whoever desires to become great among you, let him be your servant. And whoever desires to be first among you, let him be your slave— just as the Son of Man did not come to be served, but to serve, and to give His life a ransom for many" (Bible Gateway).

I have prophetic power and understand all mysteries and all knowledge and if I have all faith, so as to remove mountains, but have not love, I am nothing."[11] Paul is saying not just to leaders, but to all those who are called to be the salt of the earth, if we have all the knowledge and the brilliance in the world, but do not have love, then what we do is worthless. While Collins does not explicitly say love is the key; however, he notes, right direction starts with right leadership character.

Practical Application

Twenty-first century leadership must embrace the principle of participation, getting people involved, this is what Collins believes is one primary aspect of achieving greatness. Leadership is not a one-person task. The old adage says, "If a leader looks behind them and no one is there, he or she is not leading, they are simply just giving orders." The principle of participation seeks new ways of rallying and mobilizing people to come together for a common purpose; rather than staying stuck to grass root ideals. Christian leaders who are seeking greatness in the church today, must be willing to preach and teach with relevancy, and maintain an openness and approbation for diversity in: people, gifts, talents and ideals. Leaders must be willing to seek innovative choices for old churches. It is important to know, seeking innovative ways of doing church does not mean abandoning the faith. While there are non-negotiables in many facets of life, there are non-negotiables in the church. Since new ideas sometimes produces fear in those needing to make change, then leaders provide congregants with the appropriate trainings and teachings relevant to helping the church grow and become the body of Christ intended from its origin; altogether great in the sight of God.

---

[11] Bible Gateway Online. October 25, 2016.

Theology Of Leadership

This writer promotes a theology of leadership that seeks to make leaders aware that futuristic leadership is vital to the revitalization of the church. What does futuristic mean? According to the Cambridge dictionary, futuristic means, a strange and very modern, intended or seeming to come from imagined time in the future.[12] In other words, having a futuristic view is a view that looks ahead of time; looking at a future view of the world. Why is it important to exercise a leadership with futuristic lenses? This is important because statistics show that church membership continues to decline by the thousands yearly much because people do not feel church is relevant to their everyday life situations. Therefore, this writer embraces a futuristic leadership that (1) possesses relevant visions (2) prepares and calls the church to action and (3) possesses great faith.

There are many people who are afraid of thinking about the future. The thoughts of uncertainty seem to cripple them. But, in all actuality, movement, whether we embrace it or not, it is always occurring. Things are always evolving and changing. Since movement is evident in life, experts urge people to find purpose which makes life meaningful. Sacred text echoes this sentiment noting, without a vision people perish.[13] One definition of the word, vision in the Cambridge Dictionary is the ability to imagine how a country, society or industry or other sects will develop in the future and to plan in a suitable way. This person is called a visionary. Leaders are called visionaries. They are visionaries because they have been called to order the life of the church not just for the present, but they must look beyond the pews and see the church outdoors. This is in part the commission, go into all the world and make disciples (Matthew 28: 18-20).

---

[12] Cambridge Dictionary Online

[13] New International Version. Proverbs 29:18.

As leaders who are primarily responsible for growing the church and growing other leaders, leaders must write the vision. When Habakkuk was angry because Israel was going contrary to God's law, God told the prophet three things: (1) write the vision, (2) make it plain and, (3) post it up high. The reason for these precise instructions were so that those who saw the vision could read the vision and run with it. In other words, carry the vision out. This what Christian leadership must be doing so that the church will know where they going and what they are being called to do.

Not only should leaders be visionaries as futuristic leaders, but they must be ready to respond to present and impeding future situations. Futuristic leadership looks at current world situations and develops plans for how the church needs to respond as being the body of Christ. Carl S. Dudley in *Where Have All Our People Gone?* notes, it is imperative that Christian leaders and pastors prepare congregants for ministries that help them rightly respond to world situations. Teaching people is an unending task as leaders and a requirement for pastors according to sacred text: (1 Timothy 3:2). The Bible admonishes qualified leaders to teach sound doctrine. Leaders are further admonished to teach because the flock needs guidance in making appropriate steps. Since as Christians, the greatest teacher was Jesus, Christian leaders should be compelled to emulate Jesus's ministry. While leaders look back to understand Jesus' ministry, they can simultaneously look forward to leading and preparing people for the world in which they exist.

When considering leadership as a futuristic endeavor, John the Baptist's ministry serves as a great example, as he was preparing people for the future; the coming of Christ. Not only did John the Baptist prepare people for the future, but Jesus rebuked people who failed to look forward. Luke records Jesus scolding the crowd for not being able to recognize the times: saying "'Hypocrites! You know how to interpret the appearance of the earth and the sky, but why don't you know how to interpret this time'

(Luke 15: 56)?" In essence, it is the responsibility of leadership to help the flock know how to interpret the time and rightly respond.

Lastly, a futuristic view of leaders embraces and understands the need to possess great faith. The Bible teaches, faith is the substance of things hoped for, the evidence of things not seen. Another translation states, "'Now faith is the confidence in what we hope for and assurance about what we do not see' (Hebrews 11:1)." In essence, faith proceeds what is seen. Faith in essence is futuristic. Faith is much like grace. Grace goes ahead of humanity, it meets each of us at every place and every corner of life.

Hence, leadership demands forward movement and forward looking. Leaders must start with the end in mind. Starting with the end is mind is called the Backward Design. Habakkuk demonstrates a leadership that demanded faith. Although God was silent, not responding to Habakkuk's complaints and laments; yet, he knew God would take action, stating: "'I will stand my watch and set myself on the rampart, and watch to see what he will say to me' (Habakkuk 2)." A New Testament example of faith in action is that of the Centurion who Jesus notes had great faith. The Centurion's faith was so great that it resulted in his slave being healed by Jesus without Jesus ever being in the slave's presence. The great faith of the Centurion resulted in change for someone else. The faith of futuristic leadership helps shape the lives those lead.

In leadership there are times when leaders must step out in faith believing and putting ministries and leaders in place, preparing people for the now and the later. Futuristic leadership as Collins notes cannot be motivated by fear, but yet stay true to its core values. If Christian leadership desires to stay to its core values and beliefs then, leadership must be willing to face some hard facts about future leading and what the church will look like if leadership is only relevant to those in one generation. Futuristic leadership is willing face the brutal facts, think discipline thoughts and take discipline actions.

In essence, leadership does not seek to be served, but rather seek to serve. Seeking to serve in a futuristic view of leadership causes one to look beyond the Sunday morning pews; seeing the generations to come. And, in seeing the future generations, futuristic leaders identify ministries that will mentor, grow and prepare people beyond the here and now. In focusing on generations to come, Betsy Schwarzentraub in *Afire with God* writes, "looking ahead means doing good for generations to come altogether; using our money, passions, time, abilities and assets wisely."[14]

In other words, looking ahead means preparing for members of the Post-modern Generation known as the: Gen Xers, Busters or Thirteeners. Thus, opening the doors and connecting with those who are outside the church. Futuristic leaders seek innovative ways to be the church both inside and out. Overall, I believe the key to advancing God's Kingdom in the earth and truly being the body of Christ is linked to a futuristic view of leadership. Futuristic leadership seeks, mobilizes, educates, finds the needy, looks for the oppressed, brings back the lost, feeds the hungry, ministers to the hurting. This is truly the church all of which is tied to futuristic leadership.

---

[14] Schwarzentraub, Betsy. Afire with God. Equipping the Future Church. National Council of Christian Churches. 1989.

THE CREATIVITY OF BIBLE STUDIES

Minister Derrick Wayne Webster
Oak Ridge First Baptist Church
Oak Ridge, North Carolina

One of the tragic ills life brings to all Christians is the concept of what is relevant and what is not relevant? One might wrestle with this notion in their daily lives in order to cope, cooperate and co-exist in the arena called life. Tim Stevens, author of "Pop Goes the Church," and executive pastor at Granger Community Church, has an interesting viewpoint of relevance. He states "Relevance is all about being missional. You are studying the culture and figuring out what works. The goal is to communicate. So you figure out what it takes to communicate (either one-on-one or in a group setting) to the people in front of you." I whole-heartedly concur with Tim and this leads me to implore my peers in ministry to be aware of the present age that we teach the engrafted Word of God.

Before I go any further, I must be intentional by letting leaders and laity be keenly aware every model discussed in this chapter has to be tailored to meet the needs of their local assemblies. One of the things I love about Jesus as he diligently traveled throughout his 33 and a half years on earth was how he taught relevant lessons for each audience.

Did Jesus conform to the crowd? Absolutely not! He best exemplified what Paul said in 1 Corinthians 9:22-23 "to win all." If Jesus wasn't missional, then I have no earthly idea who was. As a matter of fact, his mission was such until he fulfilled it through death on the cross. "For God So Loved the World that he gave his only begotten Son that whosoever believes in him should not perish but hath everlasting life"-John 3:16. Understanding this, one has to ask themselves the question how do we stay relevant when it seems that irrelevance has taken the day.

This became real to me one day in my own life as a pastor's son. I knew Scripture from like the old saints used to say from "kibber to cover." To be honest, I didn't quite know what that meant, but all I knew was it sounded like I knew a lot. The challenge came, as Paul also said in 1 Corinthians 13:11," when I became a man I put away childish things," and I realized I couldn't appropriately associate Scripture to the right areas in my life. This caused me to do some deep soul searching and to ask God for guidance on how to make his word practical and relevant to my everyday situations.

One of the most critical things that could ever be said of someone is they have the information but they do not understand the application.

One of the most critical things that could ever be said of someone is they have the information but they do not understand the application. This is a good time to make the announcement this is where many of our ministries are at this time. We have information, but we fall short on the application of it to make it relevant. In my searching, God revealed to me a plan to look at biblical characters and ask myself the question "what you would do if you were in these biblical character's shoes?" I distinctively remember reading Daniel Chapter 3 and saying, "I think if I would have been Shadrach, Meshach or Abednego I would have bowed because I do not like heat!!!!" Well of course the spirit in me burned with conviction for thinking that way because if anyone who professes they love God and know his word should not take this route. What would happen to the world he left us to help bring salvation to others? It was at this moment I asked God to give me insight, wisdom and knowledge to make his word relevant.

I will use the story of Shadrach, Meshach and Abednego (a.k.a. the Hebrew boys) as an example of making a Bible story relevant.

We must understand when we ask anything according to his will, he will hear us 1 John 5:14. These Hebrew boys showed me several things I'd like to share as we discover the authenticity of relevant Bible studies. The first example of relevancy is when you make a declaration, of being confident about whom you are serving or you will be put under fire. They said in Chapter 3:16-17 they were not careful (meaning not biting my tongue; saying what I mean, and meaning what I say to King Nebuchadnezzar). They were saying in effect "I would rather take a chance with my God because even if God did not deliver me from the fire, it would not mean that God could not deliver me." In essence, bowing down to an earthly king or god has no relevance in my life because I know how strong my God is. They emphasized the fact that regardless, they would not serve his golden image as stated in vs.18.

Relevancy took form again in this text when these young men resolved that if they were not going to bow, it would anger this King and they would have to suffer the consequences. King Nebuchadnezzar commanded his men to heat up the furnace seven times hotter. Well, to the average casual reader, the number seven would not mean much. However, in trying to make it relevant to congregants we as leaders have to stress the importance that seven is God's perfect number. With that being said, sometimes what the enemy seems for evil, God makes it just right for his power to be manifested.

It was when the furnace temperature was raised seven times hotter; God used what Nebuchadnezzar meant to devour his saints as a method to make them stronger, wiser and better as Marvin Sapp wrote in his lyrics "Never would have made it."

The Bible says even the men the king ordered to put them in the furnace were devoured according to verse 22. Why is this relevant? It is relevant to note when you make a stand for God and a stand against powers that be, those who try to throw you in the furnaces of life will be destroyed. If this wasn't enough, the king looked in the furnace and saw the three Hebrew boys bound in the furnace, he saw someone else. This someone else he described being with them in vs.25 was the Son of God whom actually hadn't been born yet.

When I taught this lesson to a group of believers, I told them this best displayed why Jesus came to earth. He came not only to save, to deliver and to set free, but to also torment and to destroy the works of the devil according 1John3:8. Jesus will always show up before he is ever needed.

Now the text doesn't say this and I do not want to commit "Hermeneutic Homicide," but I concur this Scripture shows us the Hebrew boys were loosed according to vs.27 and the fire had no power on them. This says when we make a stand; we won't look like what we've been through. And it also implies as we try to reach this present age with practical relevant teachings, we serve a God who won't always keep us from the fire but we do serve a God who will keep us in the fire.

In my exegetical summation of this text I believe God also shows us these men came out of the fire but the fourth man stayed in the fire. I believe He stayed in the fire so we, who have to go in the fires of life, will have Him there for us just like He was for them.

What am I saying through all of this? I'm trying to relay to all 21st century pastors, leaders, Sunday School teachers, deacons, saints and friends, as we used to say in the African American tradition of worship, if we are to be relevant and practical in our presentations of biblical studies not only should we know the story but we must also be able to portray the glory that shall be revealed in present day terms, as products of tests, trials and temptations real people face everyday.

I will be the first to admit this is sometimes mind boggling because we have to get past our own insecurities and insufficiencies and rely on what Paul said of all he learned as dung in Philippians 3:8. Now let me be clear this doesn't mean we should not be learned individuals, because we should know more now than ever before.

During a conversation with Dr. Sir Walter Mack, the collaborator of this book, he shared his views on economic development and community revitalization from a continuing education program at Harvard University. Dr. Mack was also a guest lecturer and round table participant at Oxford University in Oxford, England, which focused on the role of religion in education and the government. He currently serves eight students as their academic advisor and theological mentor through the doctoral program at United Theological Seminary which focuses on developing leadership for effective programming ministry in the Post-Modern Era.

Most importantly, he shared with me and some other fellow peers that with all of his training, he needs to go back to school because what he has is outdated. I looked at him as if he had lost his mind or was having a nervous breakdown. Let me be clear, he wasn't saying what he has is not adequate but he was saying in order to stay relevant and effective in giving people biblical solutions and accuracy for today's ills and vicissitudes which try to hinder, hamper and halt our walks with God, we have to stay in the academy of learning with precision and consistency.

That conversation led me to consider where I am, and caused me to come to the conclusion I also need further instruction to deal with a godless generation in whom we sometime alienate because we don't make what we do and say relevant. My point is not everybody will be able to go to Harvard, Elon, Duke, Shaw or United Theological, but everyone has access to literature, libraries, and learning retreats which can help make your teaching and reaching relevant to a post-modern era.

I teach a contemporary and comprehensive Bible study every Tuesday Night at the Oak Ridge First Baptist Church which encompasses every age group within our ministry. It reaches for relevance through clarity and clenching teaching of the Scriptures. I will go on record and say any ministry that doesn't strive to be relevant will be relinquished. This would be a tragedy to the world we live in and the communities by which we serve to be relieved of our duties as the voice of God.

My pastor and father, Dr. James A. Webster once said John the Baptist was a voice crying out in the wilderness, and now it seems we have a wilderness crying out for a voice. I add to what my pastor says by saying the voice the world is crying for is one of that is relevant and includes being relational. This has to do with our connectedness, or relentless which has to do with our being steady and persistent, and/or relegating, which has to do with the church coming to a seemingly lower position to become approachable.

Jesus, if you will, in order to make His teaching relevant was often criticized for dining with sinners and publicans like he did in Matthew 9:10 and going home with tax collectors like Zaccheus. One of my mentors, Dr. Cardes H. Brown, Pastor at New Light Baptist Church, Greensboro, North Carolina told me one day people do not want to know what you know until they know how much you care. I thought much of this and this helps me prepare for relevant Bible studies every time I must present. Part of our problems is people can't identify with our gospel we teach because we haven't yet identified with our surrounding cultures. Every culture is different whether you're in the inner city or in the rural area, but the bottom line is we've be called to be relevant and that's why we have to be creative in our Bible study presentations.

I want to close this chapter by sharing some successful methods I found work with making Bible study relevant. I call it the 3C-Plan. The 3C-Plan first of all has to do with making biblical presentations CLEAR. One day I was reading a work on Focus on the Family by Robert Velarde, a writer, philosopher and author. He suggested if we don't know how to interpret God's message to us then we will become confused and probably end up misinterpreting biblical content. In being clear we have to keep biblical context of which we teach. Velarde also suggests related to biblical interpretation is a concept known as perspicuity. In short, the term means the Bible is always clear when it comes to communicating truths about the essentials of the faith. This is where biblical teachers of the faith have to be sure of making we are hermeneutically on point. If we are to be true to 2 Timothy 2:15, which tells us to study to shew thyself approved, a workman that needeth not to be ashamed, rightly dividing the word of truth, we must be clear in allowing the Spirit of God to help us to interpret what is being said not only for then but for now and even the future.

The second principle in order to make Bible study relevant is to be CONCISE. This has to do with where we give a lot of information clearly and in a few words. I must admit I'm not always disciplined in this area but I work on it daily. Sometimes we have to understand people will grasp what we teach in a shorter time effectively, than they would us in a larger time frame with little to no effectiveness at all. My grandfather, the late Deacon James Edward Webster, affectionately know as "Tom Webster" used to say, "It don't take God all day to do nothing." I didn't understand at first but I do now Grandpa and I say Amen to your words. I also add if it doesn't take God all day it should not take us all day either. To give you a little joke I heard; One day a preacher was getting up to teach and his wife kept looking at him, blowing a kiss and saying it as she did it. She kept saying K-I-S-S at least 3 times. When he was done he said, "honey you got me excited when you kept blowing and saying K-I-S-S." She said, "yes I know but you still didn't get it." He said, "what do you mean?" Her response was "I was telling you to Keep-It-Short-Stupid." Now I'm not suggesting anyone is a stupid individual but I will say when we take forever to give a relevant word through biblical teachings it is overwhelming and a bit much to the hearers. With that understood there's always a blessing in brevity. Enough said.

Our last principle in order to make Bible study relevant is to be CREDIBLE. How do we do this? CREDIBLE is the idea of where we convince the hearers we are convinced of what we are convicted and governed by ourselves. Relevant Bible studies have to be based on the power of the Word of God and not in our own demonstrations. Paul teaches us his speech was not with enticing words of man's wisdom but in demonstration of the Spirit and power in 1 Corinthians 2:4. What does this say to laity and laymen alike? It says the word is credible all by itself and we don't have to prove it, but it has to approve us. It is so credible it was fed to lions but they couldn't swallow it, placed in fiery furnaces as I said before but could not be burned up, bound in chains but couldn't be held in bondage, shipwrecked but not without an anchor, crucified on a cross, but only to rise 3 days later with all power in heaven and earth. It is this credibility that must be taught and made relevant to believers so they may grow thereby as Peter says in 1 Peter 2:2 with the sincere milk of the word that there might be piety in the heart which is susceptible of growth.

THE CREATIVITY OF A CHRISTIAN DANCE PARTY

Dr. Kevin D. Sturdevant

Grooms Chapel Church

Reidsville, North Carolina

Of the many animated movies my kids enjoy, the Shrek series has to be their favorite. We have several of the action figures and own all of the movies on DVD. Any time one of the movies is on TV, we sit down and watch it with tip-toe anticipation as if it were our first viewing. By far my children's favorite part of the first Shrek movie is the end. Not because of the movie's insistence on finding the best in someone and not because in the end good vanquishes evil. My children's favorite part is the end, because in the end they get to dance.

As the movie concludes, there is a dance sequence in which all the main characters come together in a party atmosphere to dance and sing to Smash Mouth's version of "I Believe." Inevitably, as the movie ends, my kids will all look at me and ask, "Daddy, can we dance?"

With my permission, up from the couch they leap, twisting, turning and tumbling with uncontainable enthusiasm about what they've just seen and experienced. Maybe they're just tired of sitting still and have ants in their pants. Maybe they dance in a way to express what their words cannot say. Or maybe they dance because there is something innate in us that calls and causes us to dance when no other form of expression will do.

In these moments, in the privacy of our own home, my children have the blessed opportunity to experience something many other Christians don't have – the joy of dance. For many in the African-American church community, dance has been confined and constricted to the liturgical dance that takes place during worship service or the exulting and exhilarating Holy Ghost two-step that can result from a Word received in due season. But what about a specified time and place outside of the traditional worship experience in which we can just dance? Is there any room on life's dance floor for the Christian? Is there place in Christendom to just dance?

I have personally seen the spiritual fruit from dancing in a non-traditional atmosphere and believe there is a role amongst the saints of God for Christians to have dance parties.

I have personally seen the spiritual fruit from dancing in a non-traditional atmosphere and believe there is a role amongst the saints of God for Christians to have dance parties. I never shall forget my first "Jesus Jam" as a college student at North Carolina A&T State University. In a dimly lit room in the Student Union, I and several of my friends danced on a Friday night. While many other students were dancing to R. Kelly and Boys II Men, my Christian friends and I danced to Kirk Franklin and John P. Kee. We didn't dance to show who had the best dance moves. We didn't dance because we wanted to be seen. In a way, we danced to show that Christians can have fun too. And at the end of the dance after the DJ played the last song, he offered Christ to anyone there who was lost and two people received Jesus at night – loud Christian music blaring and all. I liken my experience at Jesus Jam that night to the wedding feast at Cana of Galilee.

If there's any place in Scripture where the joy of life and excitement of the future spilled over in public praise and perhaps dancing it would be at Jesus' first miracle at the Wedding of Cana in John 2. There the Bible says:

> And the third day there was a marriage in Cana of Galilee; and the mother of Jesus was there: ²And both Jesus was called, and his disciples, to the marriage. ³And when they wanted wine, the mother of Jesus saith unto him, They have no wine. ⁴Jesus saith unto her, Woman, what have I to do with thee? mine hour is not yet come. ⁵His mother saith unto the servants, Whatsoever he saith unto you, do it. ⁶And there were set there six waterpots of stone, after the manner of the purifying of the Jews, containing two or three firkins apiece. ⁷Jesus saith unto them, Fill the waterpots with water. And they filled them up to the brim. ⁸And he saith unto them, Draw out now, and bear unto the governor of the feast. And they bare it. ⁹When the ruler of the feast had tasted the water that was made wine, and knew not whence it was: (but the servants which drew the water knew;) the governor of the feast called the bridegroom, ¹⁰And saith unto him, Every man at the beginning doth set forth good wine; and when men have well drunk, then that which is worse: but thou hast kept the good wine until now. ¹¹This beginning of miracles did Jesus in Cana of Galilee, and manifested forth his glory; and his disciples believed on him.

When one looks at this text, dancing is nowhere to be mentioned. The text doesn't indicate Jesus ever cut a rug, or stepped in the name of love, but a close examination of the context of the Scripture may bring the particulars of this wedding party into closer view. First, we must understand they danced because it was part of their culture. It was part of the Jewish culture for there to be dancing at wedding feasts. In fact, a study of wedding feasts indicates they could "last as long as seven days" and include "speeches, dancing, skipping, prayer and of course food." But this dancing wasn't just any type of dancing. This circle dance was called the horah and was "danced at least several times during the wedding reception, this lively circle dance encourages participation by everyone." Historically, everyone would have been encouraged to dance, including Jesus and His disciples.

Not only is dancing part of Jewish culture it is also part of African-American culture. In his book, Black Church Beginnings, Henry H. Mitchell, points out once African slave masters discovered the power and effectiveness of communication through dancing and drumming the slave masters banned both practices and labeled them as sinful. Could it be our current view of shunning dance outside of the shouting or worship context originated as a practice to stunt and stifle our ancestors from expressing themselves in spiritual ways? Even though our ancestors were discouraged to dance, they danced anyway under the dark of night and in secluded places knowing, as Dr. James Forbes once remarked, that "heaven is equipped to receive choreographed prayer."

Dancing as a part of the culture in and of itself or just because everyone else is doing it makes us no more than senseless robots. Those at the party who were connected to the wedding party would also have been dancing, secondly, because of the care Christ showed in their situation. In antiquity, it would have been considered highly inconsiderate, embarrassing and even a cause for litigation to not be able to provide for all the guests at a wedding feast. That's why Jesus' mother sprung into action and asked Him to intervene. And when He did, He showed He cared for the reputation of those who were throwing the feast. Can you imagine the uproar that would have followed the announcement the wine would not continue to flow? Jesus cared and just because He cared it was cause to dance.

If there was ever a reason to throw a Christian dance party, that would be it. Not just to dance because the rent is paid, not just to dance because of a positive diagnosis, not just to dance because of a new house or a big bonus on the job, but just because He cares. The Lord cares. If Jesus cares enough about the fall out of embarrassment that may result from a shortage of wine at a wedding feast, you know he cares about the embarrassment you may be facing in your own personal crisis. If Jesus cares about the amount of grapes in your glass, he cares about the amount of groceries in your cupboard. The fact He cares causes me to dance because since He cares He will comfort.

Culture and caring should be enough for us to throw a dance party.

Culture and caring should be enough for us to throw a dance party, but lest we forget there is one reason and one reason only the wedding feast in Cana happened in the first place. Celebration! Those in attendance at the wedding of Cana were there to celebrate the union of a bride and groom. They were there to celebrate the couple's coming together and their future together. And so they danced in celebration.

That's why there's room for a Christian dance party. You and I as Christians need to dance in celebration. Whether married or single, whether young or old, whether rich or poor – we should dance in celebration of the union between sinner and Savior, mankind and Mercy and the guilty and Grace! We are the Bride of Christ. What a wonderful reason to celebrate and dance. We didn't deserve to wear the white gown, but His righteousness bought it for us. We didn't deserve the promise ring of a covenant relationship with God, but His righteousness bought it for us. We didn't deserve to have our futures secured in eternity, but His righteousness bought it for us.

The Bible helps us to understand that unlike my kids after a showing of Shrek we already have permission from our Daddy to dance. Psalm 150:4 reminds us to praise Him with the timbrel and dance. Ecclesiastes 3:4 reminds us there is a time to mourn and a time to dance. Psalm 149 encourages us to rejoice and praise His name in the dance. And so, there's only one thing left to do.

In August of 2010, I heard an interesting story on National Public Radio that shed light on the importance of our dancing because of culture, care and celebration. At that time, the number one club banger in Nairobi, Kenya was a song called "Kupe de Kalle (Tobina) by artist Daddy Owen. Interestingly enough this song is a Gospel song. According to MTV Africa host VJ Kule "Kupe de Kalle is the sort of song you'd find men dancing to in a nightclub at 3 in the morning." The interviewer asked VJ Kule why the song is so popular even in nightclub settings and he said Tobina means to dance. In essence, the draw of the song is after God has blessed you, brought you out and healed your body – there's only one thing left to do – Dance. So let's dance. Let's dance in the sanctuary. Let's dance in the firmament of his power. Let's dance in dorm rooms and church basements. Let's dance in Christian night clubs. Wherever you are, the dance floor is open and the Holy Spirit is asking for your dance.

THE POLITICS OF JESUS AND CREATIVITY

Dr. Herbert Miller

Metropolitan Tabernacle Church

Flint, Michigan

Mark 11.27-33

We live in a day and age that the life of Jesus has been misconstrued, misunderstood and misinterpreted. Some Christians have decided not to participate in the political processes of this country because they have come to believe our faith tells us not to. Today, we sometimes hear this discussion on the separation of church and state. I personally believe, this is used by those who are not people of faith to keep those who are people of faith from participating in the political process. What is even more problematic is we as people of faith have heard this idea of separation of church and state bandied around so much that many of us have come to believe they are correct.

If I could, I would like to free the church by telling you exactly what the separation of church and state is. The separation of church and state comes from a letter written by Thomas Jefferson to the Danbury Baptists Association in 1802 where he says, "I contemplate with sovereign reverence that act of the whole American people which declared that their legislature should 'make no law respecting an establishment of religion, or prohibiting the free exercise thereof,' thus building a wall of separation between church and state."

Jefferson's mindset appears in our constitution as follows. The First Amendment simply says, "Congress shall make no law respecting an establishment of religion, or prohibiting the free exercise of..."

Nowhere does it say religion must always be separated from political or governmental affairs. It says the government does not have the power to establish a religion or to keep you from practicing your religion. People have taken this statement and twisted it so until many people believe it prohibits religion, and it does not.

> *When we take a serious, honest look at Jesus, who lived in first century Palestine, and see him through the eyes of his contemporaries, we begin to see a different Jesus.*

The church has not taken a stand on this issue in the past and that is how they were able to take prayer out of schools. Plato once said, "The penalty that good men pay for not being interested in politics is to be governed by men worse than themselves."

If the church decides to remove itself from the realm of politics, this country is doomed to self-destruct.

When we take a serious, honest look at Jesus, who lived in first century Palestine, and see him through the eyes of his contemporaries, we begin to see a different Jesus. We find that Jesus was a liberator. He preached and practiced liberation. He preached deliverance from social constraints and people that kept others from living in the abundance of life. Liberation theology is always political.

That is why the chief priests, the scribes, the elders and others questioned Jesus' authority. He spoke with spiritual authority, but he also spoke with political authority that incurred practical implications. Christianity at its best is about feeding the hungry, clothing the naked, and looking out for the oppressed. How do you do that without being political? The poor and the oppressed were the overwhelming majority in Palestine. The good news of the "kingdom" of God was news about the future state of affairs on earth when the poor would no longer be poor, the hungry would be satisfied, and the oppressed would no longer be miserable.

The "kingdom" that Jesus talked about is a thoroughly political notion. It is a society in which the political structure is monarchical, that is to say, it is ruled and governed by a king. Nothing that Jesus ever said would lead one to think that he might have used this term in a non-political sense. In the society that Jesus lived in, money was the second most important value. The dominant value was prestige. In the oriental world to this day, prestige is more important than any other factor and people will commit suicide rather than forfeit it.

In Jesus' day, a constant recognition of status was essential. People lived off the honor and respect which others gave them. Status and prestige were based upon ancestry, wealth, authority, education and virtue. Status was just as much a part of religion as it was part of social life. That's why Jesus' enemies always brought up the subject of his ancestry and family history.

But Jesus flat out contradicted all of this. He saw it as one of the fundamental structures of evil in the world and he dared to hope for a "kingdom" in which such distinctions would have no meaning. As you can see, Jesus had no choice but to be involved in politics. He fought a political fight on two fronts; he fought against the Romans political oppression of his people and the Pharisees, Sadducees, and religious elite's religious-political oppression of their own people.

We must remember that there was no supposed "separation of church and state" in first century Palestine. Religion was political and politics was religious; they all ran together.

Let's take a moment to examine the politics of Jesus.

I. WHAT WERE SOME OF THE POLITICAL STATEMENTS JESUS MADE?

- In Matthew 10:26, Jesus is giving his disciples advice on how to operate in the world. He says to them, "So have no fear of them; for nothing is covered up that will not be uncovered, and nothing secret that will not become known. What I say to you in the dark, tell in the light; and what you hear whispered, proclaim from the housetops. Do not fear those who kill the body but cannot kill the soul; rather fear him who can destroy both soul and body in hell."

  He goes on to say, "Everyone therefore who acknowledges me before others, I will acknowledge before my Father in heaven; but whoever denies me before others, I will also deny before my Father in heaven."

  This was a political statement, because he was either talking about the Romans who occupied the country at this time or the Pharisees, Sadducees, scribes and elders.

- In Matthew 15:26, Jesus told the Canaanite woman, "It is not fair to take the children's food and throw it to the dogs." When Jesus called this lady a dog, it was a political statement. He was supporting the current race relations and foreign policy of the Jews. This woman was a Canaanite and a gentile. They had no dealings with these people because they were considered unclean because of their mixed heritage.

- In Matthew 19:23, Jesus makes another political statement. He says, "Truly I tell you, it will be hard for a rich person to enter the kingdom of heaven. Again I tell you, it is easier for a camel to go through the eye of a needle than for someone who is rich to enter the kingdom of God."

- Then, just in case that wasn't political enough for you, just a few verses later he makes a statement that no one can doubt is political. He says, "Truly I tell you, at the renewal of all things, when the Son of Man is seated on the throne of glory, you who have followed me will also sit on twelve thrones, judging the twelve tribes of Israel. And everyone who has left houses or brothers or sisters or father or mother or children or fields, for my names sake, will receive a hundredfold, and will inherit eternal life. But many who are first will be last, and the last will be first."

Jesus says he will be seated on his throne, ruling Jerusalem, his disciples will rule with him, and those who are now first will be last. It doesn't get any more political than that.

- In Luke 13:31b-34a, the Pharisees told Jesus, "Get away from here, for Herod (the king) wants to kill you." Listen to what Jesus says about the king. He said, Go and tell that fox for me, 'Listen, I am casting out demons and performing cures today and tomorrow, and on the third day I finish my work. Yet today, tomorrow, and the next day I must be on my way, because it is impossible for a prophet to be killed outside Jerusalem.' Jerusalem, Jerusalem, the city that kills the prophets and stones those who are sent to it!'" Jesus talks blatantly to the king and lambasts the city of Jerusalem. It's hard to take an honest look at the statements Jesus made and not think he was political.

II. THOSE ARE SOME OF THE POLITICAL STATEMENTS JESUS MADE, BUT LET'S LOOK AT SOME OF JESUS' POLITICAL ACTIONS.

- In Matthew 17:24-27, we find Jesus participating in the political process. The collectors of the temple tax came to Peter and asked, "Does your teacher not pay the temple tax." They were always trying to use the political structures to hem Jesus up. Peter said, "Yes, he does."

Jesus told Peter, "What do you think, Simon? From whom do kings of the earth take toll or tribute? From their children or from others?"

When Peter said, "From others." Jesus said to him, "Then the children are free. However, so that we do not give offense to them, go to the sea and cast a hook; take the first fish that comes up; and when you open its mouth, you will find a coin; take that and give it to them for you and me."

- In Matthew 21:8-11, the Bible tells us Jesus makes another political statement. It says "A very large crowd spread their cloaks on the road, and others cut branches from the trees and spread them on the road. The crowds that went ahead of him and that followed were shouting, 'Hosanna to the Son of David! Blessed is the one who comes in the name of the Lord! Hosanna in the highest heaven! When he entered Jerusalem, the whole city was in turmoil, asking, 'Who is this?' The crowds were saying, "This is the prophet Jesus from Nazareth in Galilee." The city was in an uproar because they wanted to know who this king was, because people only did this for kings and dignitaries. That's why they were asking, "Who is this?"

Jesus knew this.

- Then in Luke 19, Jesus has the audacity to go and spend the day at Zaccheus' house, who was a rich tax collector. Now Jesus makes a political statement in the other direction because no self-respecting Jew or teacher of the law would have dinner with a tax collector. They did not like the tax collectors because they were working for the Roman authorities, who had conquered Jerusalem and were now occupying the country. They were also known for raising the taxes to put money in their own pockets.

- Then in Matthew 23, Jesus blasts the scribes and Pharisees publicly. He says in verses 13-15, "But woe to you, scribes and Pharisees, you hypocrites! For you lock people out of the kingdom of heaven. For you do not go in yourselves, and when others are going in, you stop them. Woe to you, scribes and Pharisees, you hypocrites! For you cross sea and land to make a single convert, and you make the new convert twice as much a child of hell as yourselves...," and he goes on and on and on.

In Luke 19.37-40, Jesus makes the ultimate political statement. He claims to be a king. There is only one problem. You cannot be a king because they already have a king.

"As Jesus was now approaching the path down from the Mount of Olives, the whole multitude of the disciples began to praise God joyfully with a loud voice for all the deeds of power that they had seen, saying, 'Blessed is the king who comes in the name of the Lord! Peace in heaven, and glory in the highest heaven!'"

"Some of the Pharisees in the crowd said to him, "Teacher, order your disciples to stop." And listen to what Jesus says. He says, "I tell you, if these were silent, the stones would shout out."

With this statement, Jesus was in essence claiming to be a king. Now that's political.

- In Luke 19.41-44, Jesus makes another political statement. He predicts the destruction of Jerusalem. He says, "If you, even you, had only recognized on this day the things that make for peace! But now they are hidden from your eyes. Indeed, the days will come upon you, when your enemies will set up ramparts around you and surround you, and hem you in on every side. They will crush you to the ground, you and your children with you, and they will not leave within you one stone upon another; because you did not recognize the time of your visitation from God." Then, right after that, he goes into the temple and began to drive out the people that the authorities had authorized to come in and sell to the people. He runs them out of the temple, even though the chief priests, the scribes and the leaders of the people had given them permission to be there. Then he says in the presence of them all, "...It is written, 'My house shall be a house of prayer"; but you have made it a den of robbers.'"

Jesus spoke truth to power. It was his politics that got him killed.

That was political. From that day forward, the chief priests, the scribes and the leaders of the people looked for a way to kill him.

Jesus spoke truth to power. It was his politics that got him killed. If you do not get involved in politics, it will severely limit your ability to get things done. Politics is where the decisions are made, the vision is cast, cities are built, communities and neighborhoods are planned, and nations are built or destroyed. It was his politics that got him killed. He ran his mouth one time too many and the powers-that-be had had enough. Politics is a rough business, but we cannot be afraid to get involved, because it is through politics that we make our community better and fight for what we believe in.

Jesus was political. His birth was political. The king was trying to kill him. I just demonstrated how his life was political. His arrest was political. Matthew 27.1-2 says, "When morning came, all the chief priests and the elders of the people conferred together against Jesus in order to bring about his death. They bound him, led him away, and handed him over Pilate the governor."

It is difficult to be a follower of Jesus the Christ and not be political.

John the Baptist was political. He had the nerve to tell King Herod he was wrong for marrying his brother's wife. Martin Luther King Jr. was political. His politics on ending the exploitation of poor people got him killed.

Jesus was political. His birth, life and arrest were political. His death was political. He was tried by Roman politicians on trumped up charges, and the politicians convicted him of high treason. The manner in which he died was political. The cross was a political statement that said to the people, "If you try to overthrow the government or fight against Roman occupation, the same will happen to you." His resurrection was political, because the politicians told the soldiers to lie about what they had seen so no one else would believe in Jesus as the Messiah.

His death was political. But, I want you to know when he comes back, that will be political too.

Revelation 19:1-16 tells us, "Then I saw heaven opened, and there was a white horse! Its rider is called Faithful and True, and in righteousness he judges and makes war. His eyes are like a flame of fire, and on his head are many diadems; and he has a name inscribed that no one knows but himself. He is clothed in a robe dipped in blood, and his name is called The Word of God. And the armies of heaven, wearing fine linen, white and pure, were following him on white horses. From his mouth comes a sharp sword with which to strike down the nations, and he will rule them with a rod of iron; he will tread the wine press of the fury of the wrath of God the Almighty. On his robe and on his thigh he has a name inscribed, "King of kings and Lord of lords."

Jesus was political. That's why I am political. I'm working, because I know he is coming back. I want to be ready when he comes...

JUST PROGRAM IT AND WATCH IT GO! *OR* I THIRST!

Reverend Latonya Oakley
Unwrapping The Gift Foundation
Oxford, North Carolina

Shortly after the death of my father I gave my life to Christ. I had come to the realization for various reasons I needed to be rescued from a life of hell. I needed a safe haven, a place of protection, somewhere to go where pain wouldn't exist. On my job I was surrounded by a lot of Christians who were not only devoted to Christ but was also devoutly dedicated to their church. After numerous invites I decided to give this church thing a try. To my surprise it was a comforting atmosphere, I enjoyed the praise and worship, meeting new people and before I knew it I was standing at the altar making a declaration that I wanted to be saved! It was the best decision that I'd ever made. As time progressed, like most new converts, I became involved in every auxiliary at my church in search of a deeper relationship with this man called Jesus. To my dismay I had become one of those devoutly dedicated Christians that I had once ridiculed.

The more that I learned about Jesus the more that I wanted to know about myself.

It was years later in my relationship with Christ I realized that it was so much more to Christianity than church attendance. The more that I learned about Jesus the more that I wanted to know about myself. It was as if I had developed what psychologist calls "the hunger factor," that intrinsic motivational drive that causes ones' behavior to change. There was something happening within me that was beyond my level of understanding. It was calling me to higher heights and deeper depths but I had no idea how to get there. I had an internal itch nothing could seem to scratch. Suddenly there was a vision of a place that seemed afar off. It was in eyesight but beyond arms length. What I was seeing it in my spirit was difficult to convey in the natural. It felt as if I were on a cruise ship in the middle of nowhere, not sure of where I was sailing to but convinced that one day I would arrive. Not having a compass was quite distressing and now I am experiencing inner turmoil. The church was responsible for this sudden awakening within my soul, but was inadequate in producing the spiritual endorphins needed to keep me afloat. It was an oxymoron, sending me to another level yet causing me to sink. I needed something more. It was at this moment I realized Spirituality was my core but it was not all of me.

Frantically as I began to search for something that would ease this yearning inside of me. I found myself running from church to church looking for that place of euphoria that would be able to satisfy this burning desire. For years I felt like the woman at the well. She ran from man to man like I ran from church to church. We were both in lieu of an experience where the ordinary just wouldn't suffice.

Abraham Maslow, a well-known psychologist believed a hierarchy of needs motivates people. Maslow's theory suggests people will pay attention to higher needs only when lower needs are satisfied. You see as my lower needs were being satisfied my expectations grew immensely. Maslow's first level consists of your physiological or your basic needs such as the need for food, water, safety, and security. Within the confines of the church, this could be metaphorically seen as salvation and then Bible basics 101. This is the place where the foundation for new converts is developed. This is when you receive your vital nutrients that stimulate spiritual growth. The second level in Maslow's hierarchy of need is the need for social interaction such as the need to belong. Contrary to how wonderful you believe your Sunday morning teachings are people often gather in church week after week because of their need for belongingness; they need something to identify themselves with. I recall the most wonderful memories and heighten sense of belongingness when I would travel with my church. Just to hear the Pastor say, "Will all of the members of my church please stand." Seeing the expression of the non-members as they looked in awe because there were so many of us and the astonishment on their faces as he preached the word were better than any social club I had affiliated myself with. In fact it was becoming my own personal social club under the leadership of Jesus Christ. For once I no longer had to fear rejection. The church was a place of acceptance for whosoever will, thus satisfying my need for social interaction. So I propose that perhaps the woman at the well was running from man to man due to a need for belongingness? Was she trying to fill a void?

This third level that Maslow suggests is the need for esteem that includes the need for respect of oneself and from others. There is no better place to learn about this than within the confines of the church. As you began to grow and adhere to the preaching and teachings of the pastor you began to develop a mutual respect for humankind. It is here where you began to value yourself, understand your struggles and the human frailties of your brothers and sisters in this walk of faith. This is the place you find acceptance as well as being held accountable for all of your decisions. This is a place of self discovery where one becomes empowered. This is a pivotal moment; a very delicate place and if not handled correctly it can be detrimental in the finding of one's purpose. It is at this place I believe many Christians become stagnant, leave the church, and begin to living contrary to what they profess; they are stuck. They have become empowered, strengthened toward their purpose, in route to their preordained predetermined destination. There are no instructions to provide them aid that will assist in reaching this climax that the church has declared everyone could have initially during Bible basics 101. So what do you do next? The woman at the well is a great illustration of this very dilemma.

⁷ A woman of Samaria came to draw water. Jesus said to her, "Give Me a drink." ⁸ For His disciples had gone away into the city to buy food. ⁹ Then the woman of Samaria said to Him, "How is it that You, being a Jew, ask a drink from me, a Samaritan woman?" For Jews have no dealings with Samaritans. ¹⁰ Jesus answered and said to her, "If you knew the gift of God, and who it is who says to you, 'Give Me a drink,' you would have asked Him, and He would have given you living water." ¹¹ The woman said to Him, "Sir, You have nothing to draw with, and the well is deep. Where then do You get that living water? ¹² Are You greater than our father Jacob, who gave us the well, and drank from it himself, as well as his sons and his livestock?"

> We need programs that are devoted to real life circumstances, programs that are designed to help individuals reach their full potential.

Here in verse 11 she is at the place where many Christians are today; she is stuck. She is so tired of the same old thing, desiring more but lacking the person, thing or program tailored for such a time as this could usher her into the last phase of Maslow's hierarchy of needs and is self-actualization, or realizing one's full potential.

This is what is needed in the 21st century church. We need programs that are devoted to real life circumstances, programs that are designed to help individuals reach their full potential. The churches are filled with help engines that teach individuals about the array of potential awaiting them; however, it is at the point of recognition we are failing. We need programs designed creatively within our churches that are tailored to the times in which young adults live. If we (the church) are not meeting the needs of our young adults they will surely gravitate towards other means of satisfaction.

This is what Jesus provided for her in John chapter 4 verses 13-15. Jesus saw the need and provided a program.

13.Jesus answered and said to her, "Whoever drinks of this water will thirst again, 14 but whoever drinks of the water that I shall give him will never thirst. But the water that I shall give him will become in him a fountain of water springing up into everlasting life." 15 The woman said to Him, "Sir, give me this water, that I may not thirst, nor come here to draw."

This young lady was thirsty and because he provided to her what she needed, it released her from the treacherous grips of the superficial enslavement of her flesh. It gave her that "experience" she had been searching for. For the first time she found purpose. She realized that it was more to her than a man; she had self-actualized.

16 Jesus said to her, "Go, call your husband, and come here." 17 The woman answered and said, "I have no husband." Jesus said to her, "You have well said, 'I have no husband,' 18 for you have had five husbands, and the one whom you now have is not your husband; in that you spoke truly." 19 The woman said to Him, "Sir, I perceive that You are a prophet. 20 Our fathers worshiped on this mountain, and you Jews say that in Jerusalem is the place where one ought to worship." 21 Jesus said to her, "Woman, believe Me, the hour is coming when you will neither on this mountain, nor in Jerusalem, worship the Father. 22 You worship what you do not know; we know what we worship, for salvation is of the Jews. 23 But the hour is coming, and now is, when the true worshipers will worship the Father in spirit and truth; for the Father is seeking such to worship Him.

Hebrews 13:8 declares Jesus Christ *is* the same yesterday, today, and forever. Although his ways are the same, his methods are not. I know we have heard the more things change the more they stay the same. Excellence is the quality of being outstanding or extremely good, however the means in which people uses to attain it will consistently change. Young people are movers and shakers, they move about in search of themselves. If we (the church) provide the vehicles (programs) in which they can use to reach maximum potential, they will offer others a ride thus creating a cycle of growth within our sanctuaries. The woman at the well had that experience and she went into the city telling everyone she met "come see a man who has told me everything." We both were in need of an experience!

IMPORTANCE OF REACHING MEN IN THE POST MODERN ERA

Pastor Derrick Horton

Impact Church

Durham, North Carolina

Scripture Focus-1 Samuel 14:6-12

Several years ago, while stationed at Ft. Bragg assigned to 1st-325th Airborne Infantry Regiment, we were scheduled to go on our Brigade run. It was early in the morning and all appeared normal. However, within minutes and without warning, shots were fired from beyond the wood line. Shocked and caught off guard a scene that moments ago was calm instantly turned chaotic. One soldier was fatally shot, twenty others wounded during this tirade of fire that lasted several minutes. The gunman was flanked by soldiers as they wrestled weapons from his hand. Staff Sgt. Anthony Minor said "we came under fire and moved into the tree line because we realized we were the only ones who could do anything about it." Could you imagine the impact as men we would have on our world when we realize, "we are the only ones who could do anything about it." If not us, who? If not now, when? I learned firsthand on that field of screams filled with surprise, chaos, and bloodshed, what happens when common men become courageous!

If we were to glance at times that predates technology, we would see common men doing courageous acts. Such is the case with Paul and Silas as two itinerant preachers who were accused of troubling the city. Moses and Aaron with steel in their spine confronted evil, oppressive, powers of a Pharaoh. Nehemiah after receiving permission from a King to diligently rebuild walls of a people was mocked and ridiculed. In each instance someone common extended, stretched, and reached beyond *maybe* into miraculous.

Which leads us to the words of Jonathan (1 Samuel 14:6 Come let us go over....it *may be* that the Lord will work)? The two books of Samuel according to Brueggemann are "lively, artistic narratives without much heavy tendentious theological overlay."[15] Take observation in this animated account of biblical action. Notice the Lord worked when they moved. Is it possible that while we are waiting on the moving of the water, the Lord is waiting for us to do something? Why sit ye' here and die asked the lepers. And when four underweight lepers decided to move, God maximized their footsteps to sound like chariots, horses, and an army (2 Kings 3-5). Peter could not walk on the water, until he moved out of the boat (Matthew 14:29). When we move, God does the miraculous.

In our text, Jonathan found himself in a long nebulous, nocturnal situation. Victorious as he was against the Philistine garrison with 1,000 troops now he finds himself, arrested by adversity. Morale had dimmed. Morale had dimmed. Weapons were non-existent. Soldiers dwindled down to a mere 600. To magnify matters Saul, his father, was King and was hiding as far as he could from any threat from the Philistines. All hope appeared lost. Lost hope, until Jonathan, decided to act!

---

[15] Bruggeremann, Walter. *An introduction to the Old Testament, pg.151.* WJK Press, 2003.

In this postmodern era, how do we regain hope that has been lost? From WWII to the present the American culture has sensed pressure. Parents are frozen with fear from school shootings. In too many instances fathers are AWOL (absent without leave). The current war against terrorism is terrorizing our economy. The reality of foreclosures, recessions, and unemployment are choking the life out of our society. Things appear to be hopeless. How do we get men involved? What are the consequences if the masses of men do nothing? How do we reach those that seem out of our reach?

From our text we learn a few things. First we see the importance of making a decision

Verse 8 *then said Jonathan, Behold, we will pass over unto these men and we will discover ourselves unto them.*

Jonathan and his armor bearer lacked advanced weaponry. There were no weapons in Israel. Their attack was not authorized from his father, the King. They were outnumbered, but we still see him making a decision. Jonathan decided to pass over. Principal meaning of the verb was to make a move or cross over. My eldest son DJ, is a basketball guru. I called him and asked, what's the purpose of a crossover? DJ says "you crossover to get space to shoot the jumper or go to the hole (basket)." While the defender may think you are one place, before he knows it you have crossed over. When common men become courageous the enemy will think we're one place.... not realizing we have crossed over. We have crossed over from the bondage of money, power, and sex. Jonathan decided to cross over and advance forward.

Let's be transparent and honest, sometimes we just don't feel like making a decision. Sometimes it's just easier to do nothing. Surrender, give up, and

Let's be transparent and honest, sometimes we just don't feel like making a decision.

tap out, wave the white flag. Yell, I'm tired and I quit! Mike Tyson says "everyone has a plan until they get hit." So, we lie stuck in the same place refusing to decide. Jonathan made a decision to move. David, after he sinned with Bathsheba had to make a decision, to be restored (2 Samuel 11). Sampson, made a decision after he was captured to call on God (Judges 16). Paul made a decision after he was blinded and knocked to the ground to receive sight from Christ and rise again (Acts 9). We find ourselves in good company. Let us decide to be better husbands, better fathers to our children. Making decisions to mentor boys, and be advocates of building our neighborhoods one block at a time. We will decide to be active in our local churches. A decision to ACT!

Secondly we learn from the text we must be willing <u>to fight on enemy territory</u>

v10 ...*if they say, come up to us, then we will go up: for the Lord has delivered them into our hand: and this shall be a sign to us.*

Jonathan and his armor bearer crawled up into a tight position before advancing. They were between two sharp cliffs. The two of them were literally, between a rock and a sharp place. Jonathan and his armor bearer give insight into crossing enemy territory. If we are going to reach men who are in hiding we must be willing to take the fight to the enemy. In 1991 a film was released starring Ice Cube, Cuba Gooding Jr, Morris Chestnut, and Laurence Fishbourne titled *Boyz n the Hood*. The movie was a gripping story of life in South Central, California. In the last scene of the movie, Ice Cube playing Doughboy after killing the men who killed his brother. While sitting on the porch, drinking a 40 oz. makes an indicting statement. Doughboy says "Either they don't know, don't show, or don't care about what's going on in the hood." Cube, was saying if they cared about the hood, they would show up. Reaching men from their hiding places to their heavenly places in Christ will require us to go where they are. There has to be a strategy that will go to meet our masses of men, where they are! Years ago, Hurricane Katrina swept through Louisiana. Ninety percent of residents flushed from their homes in Southeastern Louisiana. Nearly, 1300 people lost their lives, homes were destroyed, family structure shattered. FEMA was accused of delayed reaction. President George Bush was photographed while looking over the city from a helicopter. In the midst of tragedy, observation is useless without intervention. Men are called not to get a bird's eye view but rather an up close personal encounter. John baptized in the wilderness. Wilderness of prostitution, pimping, drug selling, and drug using. We cannot reach men where we refuse to go. Jesus reached the unreachable by going behind enemy lines. Our Master went into enemy territory when Lazarus died. Jesus said we must go back to Jerusalem. The disciples said, Master they tried to kill you. He ignored the threat and went behind enemy lines (John 11). A man in the country of the Gadarenes was out of control. Causing havoc to the nearby community Jesus went into Hostile environment. When he left, the man was clothed in his right mind (Mark 5). Jesus warned his followers, Behold I send you out like sheep among wolves (Matthew 10:16), into enemy territory. Jesus Christ was in enemy territory when He went from judgment hall to judgment hall. Enemy territory until He cried it is finished. Enemy territory when He lead captive's free.

Thirdly, we notice that leadership when <u>courageous becomes contagious</u>

v12...*Jonathan, climbed up upon his hands and upon his feet, and his armor bearer after him...*

Jonathan's bold act of courage of climbing up was emulated by his disciple. The armor bearer was able to gain and glean strength from the boldness of Jonathan, which resulted in him following after him. The inner courage that was displayed outwardly resonated within the heart of his armor bearer. He caught Jonathan's fire! Similarly Joshua caught

Moses' fire, Elisha caught Elijah's fire, Timothy caught Paul's fire and the disciples caught Jesus' fire. Mentoring is the friction that produces the spark for a fire to be lit. In Sweden in 1844 matches were made safer. Matches began coming with a unique striking force that causes a chemical reaction. The phosphorus comes in contact with potassium chlorate that's in the match head. Friction is required for ignition. General Schwarzkopf says "It doesn't take a hero to order men into battle. It takes a hero to be one of those men who goes into battle." When leadership leads from the front, it reaches the rear. Paul Laurence Dunbar poetically penned these words *"They laid them down in the valleys, they laid them down in the wood, and the world looked on at the work they did, and whispered, it is good." They fought their way on the hillside, they fought their way in the glen, and when God looked down on their sinews brown, and said, "I have made them men."*[16] We were made, Men. There has been much debate on the role of men. Charles Swindoll suggests "Over the last three decades there has been an assault on masculinity. The results are well represented in the arts, the media, the world of fashion, and among those who have become our youths' heroes."[17] We, as men have been under assault since God, first made us Men. Despite the assaults, trials, valleys, we face…our common courage must be caught!

As it relates to being common, I'm reminded of the common courage of ants. Last year, my wife informed me that we had an anthill beside our mailbox. Initially, I didn't think much of it, it's just a few ants, or so I thought. I waited about a week and to my shock the ant hill grew in just those few days. I got a broom abolished the ant hill, thinking to sweep it away. Their home was destroyed. The ants were scattered and shoved. Panic had become their reality. However, to my surprise, the ants

---

[16] Dunbar, Paul Laurence. *Selected Poems.* Unsung Heroes pg. 51 Dover Publications, 1997.

[17] Swindoll, Charles. *Man to Man* pg. 15. Zondervan Publishing House 1996.

returned. Their anthill rebuilt. The ants seemed to be a little more resilient then I first believed. Next, I got the water hose and washed away the anthill. Drowned ants were everywhere. In just a few weeks, the ants began to rebuild. The ants were determined, not to be denied even if delayed. I notified Orkin, surely a trained professional could rid my lawn of these common ants. He began to explain ants work as a team. If I sweep their home away, they will rebuild. If I drown them, the queen bee will still produce eggs, and they will eventually return. He gave me some suggestions and insight of ridding our yard from ant invasion. Thankfully, today we are ant free, but in the process I learned a valuable lesson. A common ant taught me "destroy our home, we find common courage to return and rebuild." "Sweep us out of society, we find the common courage to re-stabilize." "Drown us by the thousands, we find the common courage to still pursue."

In this postmodern era we reach men by finding, igniting, and demonstrating common courage.

CREATING A PLAN TO MOVE FROM TRADITIONALISM TO TRANSFORMATION

Dr. Rodney Coleman

First Baptist Church, Chapel Hill, North Carolina

One of my joys, as a pastor, is to witness the overall and holistic growth of my church members. This is one of the many reasons why I accepted the call to not only preach, but to pastor. I love people, and I love it when they continually reach milestones of maturity in various areas in their lives; I love to see people transform into greater versions of themselves. After all, that is why we do ministry, correct? We want to see people's lives transformed. We want to see people be better and do better. However, this process of growth and transformation is filled with various challenges, especially when the leader, who wants to see transformation, has to factor in the element of traditionalism in his or her context. What do you do, as a leader, when transformation potential, in your context, is stifled, diluted, delayed and even destroyed because of the overwhelming, and in some cases, unmovable element of traditionalism that is present and prevalent?

Many pastors have found the task of ushering and leading a church context from the valley of traditionalism to the mountaintop of transformationalism quite daunting.

Many pastors have found the task of ushering and leading a church context from the valley of traditionalism to the mountaintop of transformationalism quite daunting. This overwhelmingly concrete aspect of church methodology, rooted in traditionalism, has not only killed church growth, but killed personal member (church) growth simply because many churches refuse to change, or at best, entertain the notion of changing. This very element alone has contributed to many pastors, in many contexts, leaving parishes and congregations by astounding numbers in a quest to seek other professions altogether, or to find a context or plant a church that will embrace the element of transformation until it becomes a standard, not just "in" ministry, but also a standard "of" ministry.

Why is this? How has this overwhelming turnaround of pastoral assignments and astounding number revolving door members become the acceptable norm in many church contexts? The answer, in part, lies within understanding the element (and spirit) of traditionalism and its effect on transformation. You must understand, first and foremost, that there is a difference between tradition and traditionalism. Tradition is defined as "the transmission of beliefs or customs from generation to generation." The element of tradition, at its core, is not a bad thing. It provides foundation, history and direction. Traditions serve as a platform that support important and essential core values, and ensures that those values and cores are not forfeited and lost as generations emerge and evolve. However, when traditions are so antiquated, ineffective and non-transferable to the next generation, then those traditions need to be reassessed and reformed. The unwillingness to even entertain the reformational process enters a context and a people into the webbed world of tradition-alism- "the upholding or maintenance of tradition so as to resist change." According to Yale Historian, Jaroslav Palikan, "tradition is the living faith of the dead...traditionalism is the dead faith of the living."

When you study the life of Jesus Christ, it can be noted that even Jesus' conception was an unconventional approach from God to attack the very nature of traditionalism. After Jesus' birth, the Bible contains various examples of how Jesus tackled, attacked and addressed the elements of traditionalism while promoting the element of transformation-alism. Think about it, Jesus hangs out with sinners and tax collectors, touches lepers, advocates for marginalized women and Samaritans, speaks truth to power (Herod), and even heals on the Sabbath. Jesus was not afraid, by any means. This should not be surprising since Jesus makes it clear in Matthew 5:17 that he did not come to the earth to destroy all traditions (the law), but according to Luke 4:18-19, to restore humanity by destroying traditionalism-the maintenance and upholding of traditions that subjugated, oppressed, objectified and marginalized those who couldn't help themselves.

One example of this is found in the John 5 narrative of Jesus healing the lame man at the pool of Bethesda. Embedded within this narrative are elements of tradition and traditionalism-no work done on the Sabbath, healings that only occur in certain seasons, and the marginalized who are made to know their place and are made to believe that they must stay in their place. With one question, "will thou be made whole," Jesus chal-lenges the lame man's personal beliefs and the societal system's protocol. The answer (excuse) that the lame man gives to Jesus, in response to Jesus' question, provides insight regarding how traditionalism has fueled his outlook on life. Traditionalism has led this man to believe that hope is for-mulaic and not formative. The lame man's explanation to Jesus regarding why he has remained lame for so long is a result of him being conditioned to accept his condition. There is no record of this man using his faith and imagination to test the pool water to see if healing could occur out of the perceived season. It is my belief that this man, unlike the woman with the issue of blood, couldn't advance because he was simply conditioned by so many elements of traditionalism that it killed his ability to explore the "what ifs" that often lead to breakthroughs.

Jesus steps on the scene and commands this man to not only get up, but to "take up his mat and walk." This very command from Jesus and the following of this command, by the no longer lame man, led to a conversation and confrontation between the restored man and the Jewish leaders (by now Jesus had disappeared in the crowd). The leaders, rooted in tradition and fueled by traditionalism, question the man about why he broke the unchangeable tradition (traditionalism) of carrying his mat on the Sabbath. However, what these leaders didn't realize, when questioning the restored man, is that not only had his physical health been restored, but his mental and spiritual health. This is evident when Jesus, in another dialogue, explains to the once lame man, that transformationalism has to be a lifestyle (his new lifestyle), and the only way he would not return back to his original state (of being lame) or even something worse, was to change his ways and to live a transformative life.

This message of transformational hope only comes by leaders and agents of change.

John 5:1-15 serves as a great message and biblical foundation for many church contexts that are lame (unable to move), and unwilling to try to move because they have been conditioned to accept their conditions of comfort, conformity, complacency, or even crisis. This message of transformational hope only comes by leaders and agents of change, like Jesus, who challenge, encourage and remind those in lame contexts to pick up their beds and walk, instead of making excuses about why they are continuing to lay and die.